Pelican Books
About Chinese

Richard Newnham was born in London in 1932.
He went to Bedales and later to New College,
Oxford, where he read modern languages, in
between learning Russian at Cambridge. After two
years of journalism he joined Penguin Books as
languages editor.

He began studying Chinese in 1962, leaving with his
wife the following autumn for Hong Kong. There
he lived with a Chinese family, took more lessons,
talked with a great many students, and met Tan
Lin-tung, who helped him to draft the specifically
Chinese side of this book.

Richard Newnham returned to London, via
Peking, in 1965, and is now a director of Eyre Methuen,
the publishers.

中國語文淺説

中国语文浅说

牛恩漢　譚林通

企鵝出版社

About Chinese

by Richard Newnham

Helped by Tan Lin-tung

Penguin Books

Penguin Books Ltd, Harmondsworth,
Middlesex, England
Penguin Books Inc., 7110 Ambassador Road,
Baltimore, Maryland 21207, U.S.A.
Penguin Books Australia Ltd, Ringwood,
Victoria, Australia

First published 1971
Reprinted 1973

Copyright © Richard Newnham, 1971

Made and printed in Great Britain by
Hazell Watson & Viney Ltd
Aylesbury, Bucks
Set in Monotype Times

Contents

Acknowledgements

Other than the publishers, the only organization to encourage this book in any direct way was the China Association (*Yīng shāng zhōnghuá xiéhùi*) of the City of London. The author thanks them for a generous research bursary.

All the Chinese characters in the book were written by Tse Chi-ling.

The Chinese examples

Chinese characters and their romanized sounds are for the most part kept separate until chapter 6. This is to make easier the explanation of script and sound. Where characters occur in the early chapters, they are written in the traditional style; in chapter 6 the style is that as simplified by the communists from 1956 onwards, with the traditional form given in brackets after each simplified character. The chapter on how to write Chinese illustrates both styles.

All romanized Chinese is written in the communist *pīnyīn* system, except for a few personal names.

Where the words of an English translation are between hyphens, this means that the rendering is literal and may be compared item by item with the Chinese.

Definitions

This book is before all else an introduction to the Chinese language for non-learners. Such people may have too little time – or too much wisdom? – for a practical course in Chinese; but they would be interested in the language if it could be made to appear less remote and exotic, and on its first level the book will satisfy curiosity of this kind. Then there will be others who are prepared to become students, or prepared at least to consider the idea, given certain assurances. These readers will want an indication of the methods of learning, the time and direction of study, and the results to be expected – in short, an approach to the *idea* of learning Chinese. Finally, on its third level the book is a signpost for students already started on the language when other compass-bearings may be showing only faintly.

But what special claim has Chinese to anyone's attention? Is there any reason for wishing to be introduced, in whatever degree of involvement, to an oriental language-system?

Chinese seems to offer three perfectly good reasons. First, that acquaintance with it will bring interest and pleasure, and that both these can be lifelong rewards of an entirely unsanctimonious and indeed strenuous kind. Many have found this to be so. Second, that linguistic understanding will in some way open up the Chinese mind. The modern view of languages tends to play down all significance possibly thought to arise from their formal differences; one British scholar has compared such differences between language groups to those between various traffic systems, in that, while one country may drive on the left side of the road and another on the right, the actual vehicles, their drivers and the journeys are largely the same. Nevertheless, differences do exist and may be formulated into the Highway Code of a system of communication totally unlike that by which we ourselves drive. Something will be learnt of the native mind and thought-habit from this formulation.

The third reason for interesting oneself in Chinese is ultimately the most worthwhile of all. It concerns language reform. There is in Chinese far more to this than the somewhat academic phrase suggests – indeed it is no overstatement to say that the history of attempts at language reform is the history of modern China in miniature. Both the language and the country started in the nineteenth century from comparable positions of backwardness *vis-à-vis* the West, and both have followed much the same course since then, fraught with outside interference and inner dissension. For this odd comparison to be understood, the nature of sound and script in Chinese must be studied in broad outline at least, and with this knowledge will come an awareness not only of China's special problems as a modern nation, but also perhaps of the fact that how we communicate is often a cause of what is communicated, and that Western sounds and forms are only one medium among several.

Given that reasons for learning something about Chinese can be found, more questions arise. Which kind of Chinese? And spoken or written, or both?

As far as this book is concerned, Chinese is the so-called 'Mandarin' or 'national language'. This choice rules out any fond idea of chatting to the waiter in one's local Chinese restaurant. He will almost certainly not be from the People's Republic where Mandarin is the official language, nor from Taiwan, the island of Formosa, which also uses it. Instead he will most probably have come from Hong Kong, Singapore, or elsewhere in south-east Asia where Mandarin is still a minority language and where other varieties of Chinese (principally Cantonese) are spoken.

But then why learn to *speak* Mandarin?

Largely because it might be useful: the prospects of travel to China are far from bleak. When this book was in first draft, the Peking authorities were launched on a full-scale tourist drive, with brochures in four colours, group rates for parties of travellers, and so forth. Since then the country has had a 'cultural revolution', one of whose side-effects was a new allocation of economic priorities following the chaos early in 1967; the drive to attract foreign visitors seemed at an end. But the priorities, significantly, were economic rather than political. There is money in tourism, and, although no single word is found in Chinese that expresses the idea of voluntary travel undertaken for amusement or recreation, 'money' certainly exists. The tourists will soon reappear, their journey made easier and cheaper by growing competition among travel agencies anxious to build up the Far Eastern circuit. Business visits to China are now more frequent than at any time since 1949. Where once the trader would arrive only for the biannual Fairs, he today discovers less formal occasions and does well to follow these up in the rigorous yet unhurried atmosphere of Chinese business dealings in which the race goes to the thorough. For the businessman even a few phrases of Chinese will be useful; for the tourist they may occasionally be essential. So the situation has changed from days when a student of spoken Mandarin would probably not even have begun to learn without some urgent professional reason, such as a missionary or diplomatic posting that brought with it an entirely new and bizarre life-pattern in which the 'impossible' language would probably not be the strangest item. Nowadays no such enormous adjustments are needed, and many more people can look on Chinese as a living language like any other.

With written Chinese, the immediate usefulness of study is less easily stated, because a long explanation must first be given for the total situation to be followed. (This has been left until chapters 2 and 5.) In practical terms, any teacher of the spoken language finds it hard to keep the student away from the written characters of script, for all that the best initial results in speech may be achieved without them. The plain fact is that Western students want characters. But what are they to do with them? And what *a priori* arguments exist for studying written Chinese on its own?

Traditional Chinese literature is often said to be accessible to anyone who can read a modern newspaper, since the separate characters used in both are largely the same and have largely constant meanings. Yet – as may be guessed – Chinese literature has no more to do with its literal meaning, word by word, than has that of the West. An extensive knowledge of reference and allusion can alone begin to tell readers 'what it means'; moreover, a Chinese poem may often hinge on an ambiguity or large doubt as to how a certain character is in fact to be read, which makes nonsense of the comparison with modern journalism. For the foreigner, classical Chinese and the literary style of writing must remain specialist subjects. They require at least five years of groundwork, and this, enough time for two Western languages and their literatures to be laid open, is not willingly spared by many people. Strong arguments therefore exist for reading Chinese classics in translation and leaving the hard work to someone else.

There are those who claim to have found a high artistic or spiritual satisfaction in calligraphy without giving any great attention to lexical values. Somehow one feels that painting a picture might, as an activity, come closer to meeting such needs, for language in whatever form must surely be meaningful before all else. Calligraphy is attractive, and there is a distinct pleasure in shaping a well-balanced character on the page, but this satisfaction should remain a by-product rather than an end of study.

Our utilitarian answer to 'Why trouble with the characters?' must thus have two parts. First, that it is profitable and not too difficult to read modern Chinese written in the 'colloquial' style. As China develops, whether in isolation from the rest of the world or not, her contribution to scholarship and technology will increase and become accessible in publications. There is also good modern prose literature from the last fifty years. A reading vocabulary of about 2,000 characters can cover most contingencies in these fields.

The second part of our answer involves the pleasure-principle once again, in the attraction which characters hold for what may be termed the crossword-puzzle intellect. This mental quality is most easily judged with the help of a typology of the student of Chinese, and we shall end our brief for the language by drawing one.

A frequent objection to the idea of studying Chinese is, quite simply, that it is too difficult. In the sense that the language needs patience and considerable memorizing power, this is valid enough, but there is also some encouraging evidence which points to a measure of rough justice in the distribution of the talents such as may weigh heavily in the balance. Ability to learn and recall characters is often met with in those students who find the verbal side of language inhibiting, usually because of over-perfectionism or because they are unduly critical of their own utterances on logical grounds. Conversely the more robust spirits, gifted with a talent for mimicry and quick to catch shades of intonation and cadence, may soon have spoken fluency to compensate for their slower progress with the script or for sheer lack of interest in its visual word-shapes. Chinese may well be a lottery in which there is a prize for everyone.

*

Readers coming to this book with different aims will want different parts of it. The *non-student* should read chapters 1 to 5, which form a general account of the history of Chinese, its sounds, scripts, morphology, reforms and present state. On reaching chapter 6, he may decide to pass over its detailed information on syntax and function and turn instead to the two Chinese texts of chapter 8, looking at Mr Li's 'inside view' of the language before he gets down to them. The *potential* student, however, will find the information in chapter 6 very useful. It covers much of the dead ground between the frontiers of English and Chinese, ground which must initially be mapped even though at a later stage of study it will be rejected or unconsciously absorbed by more active learning. Finally, the *student already begun* may also want chapter 6, or some sections of it; but he should find most help in later chapters, which give advice on matters not always raised (much less answered) in the textbooks.

As for this book's method of exegesis, it makes its own rules as to how much of the truth to tell and at what moment to tell it.

Sounds   1

Language is spoken sound. As such it need have nothing to do with the ways used to transcribe sound. Yet it is often implied that, in order to speak Chinese, one must learn several thousand characters (the amounts vary) by way of a first step. Until quite recently the beginner was expected to start with the script forms. He was not asked if he wanted them, nor was it explained that *they do not transcribe sound* in the way that does a phonetic alphabet or 'romanization' (Chinese in roman letters).

Because Chinese is not a phonetic language, that is, one in which the written spelling of a word matches its spoken sound, the modern approach is via sounds alone. This is highly rational and correct. However, it can lead to another error, which is an excessive bias on the side of spoken Chinese. The paramount claims of speech may seem feeble to a student 10,000 miles from China. And after all, many people find themselves obliged to read a good deal of French without ever needing to speak it. A student in this situation with Chinese should not be intimidated into spending more time on the spoken groundwork than is necessary. He must understand the correct equation of sound with characters, and must learn the sound 'hooks' on which to hang these characters in his memory; but after that he may perfectly well concentrate on his reading. Nevertheless, whatever end is in view, the sounds must come first.

Most people will already have heard of the 'tones' before they are given a single spoken syllable in the language. It is never easy to discuss speech by writing about it, and with these tones the matter is made still harder by English terms, which do not adequately cover tonal speech. For example, subjective measurements like 'pitch' or 'level' can apply to all types of speech; if they do not isolate the meaning of a single sound, then they may convey the meaning of a whole sentence and its cadence in an otherwise non-tonal language. One result of this overlap may be the mistaken impression that Chinese tones convey shades of feeling or emphasis. In fact they do so only in certain circumstances, and then often in a way contrary to Western expectations. Strong emotion, to take one factor in speech emphasis, does not influence the tone of a particular Chinese syllable. It will ensure that the syllable is fully pronounced and not skipped over, but the tone will not change. When pronounced fully, tones are equal in their effect and do not reflect 'tone of voice'. This is hard for the Westerner to grasp, since it seems to run counter to one of the functions of speech, but the fault arises from our own poor terminology.

'Mandarin', the variety of Chinese considered here,

has four tones. These are usually named the 'high' ('first') tone, the 'high-rising' ('second'), the 'falling-and-rising' ('third'), and the 'falling' ('fourth') tone. These are tones or levels of speaking a single basic sound, rather than spellable changes within a sound. That at least is how they strike Western ears. To a Chinese, the change from, say, first to fourth tone is that from one *word* to another – as though there were an audible, tonal difference between the English 'bread' and 'bred'. So complete is the lexical change that he may even deny that the basic sound is at all the same.

As a result of sound-simplification over many centuries, spoken Mandarin today has only about 400 basic monosyllables. These, when multiplied by the four tones, put the total sound-resources of the language at rather fewer than 1,600 separate items (fewer, because some basic sounds do not in practice carry all four tones).

This is real phonetic poverty, and results in the over-crowding of meaning into sound, the frequent homophones for which Chinese is famous. Compare the situation in English. Meaningful sounds exist with 'clamp', 'clomp' and 'clump', but not as yet with 'clemp' and 'climp'. These last two are theoretically available for new coinings and could be used if there were too great a pressure elsewhere in the sound-structure of English, too many words like 'bread'/'bred' which might be confused. Chinese sounds almost never carry such 'To Let' signs. As for the tones, whatever their exact origin and linguistic function may have been (scholars disagree about this), it may at least be said that if they were intended to widen the scope of too limited a number of basic sounds, then they have not adequately done so. This is not to say that the language is disabled, or that certain things 'cannot be said' in Chinese. Nobody would use it if this were so. But given that a language may have determining factors (again an arguable point), then phonetic poverty is a most influential one.

No exact illustration of the four tones can be given, since they are in any case highly relative to each other. Their real level varies with each speaker. Most textbooks illustrate them with a graph such as the one below (degrees on the vertical axis roughly equal those of tones in the musical scale):

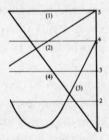

Again, parallels with the tone-level on certain English words in context are often drawn. The warning given above should be remembered: Chinese tones do not relate to dynamics but to levels in sound. Compare the level of 'home' in the following contexts:

(first tone)   'Home, home on the range' (as at the start of that song) – a high, level sound;

(second tone) 'Are you going home?' (a neutral question asked with mild interest) – evenly rising;

(third tone) 'Surely you're not going home?' (the curve of 'downwards-upwards' is often used when an English question expects the answer 'no');

(fourth tone) 'I'm going home' (a statement of finality) – flat and falling.

Translated into Chinese terms, this parallel may be seen with, for example, the basic sound *fa*. This book follows the usual practice of showing the four tones of a sound by means of four marks: *fā* (first tone), *fá* (second), *fǎ* (third), and *fà* (fourth tone). The difference between these four sounds-plus-tones, in the English example of 'home' merely one of emphasis, is now a difference of meaning, but the precise meaning may still not be pinpointed. That is, the basic sound-plus-tone may carry several lexical alternatives from which the context makes a final selection of one meaning only.

Thus, taking *fā* in use in the first tone, a Chinese-English dictionary may give one generalized definition ('to start, promote, issue'), which as it happens is the only lexical connotation for the syllable in that tone. With this will appear a list showing *fā* in use in this sense, but with other sounds that are commonly linked to it more (or less) closely. A Chinese will seldom be heard to say '*fā*' on its own, since like the majority of syllables it has a tendency to coalesce with others and to produce a wide range of associated ideas. For *fá* in the second tone there will be four or five definitions, plus the associates. *Fă* will have two, while the fourth tone *fà* is mostly kept for borrowed foreign words which are translated phonetically into Chinese sound-equivalents, such as 'fascism', 'France', etc., where '*fà-*' gives the first syllable its sound-value.

There need not be any link of a derivative or relative kind between the meanings attached to the four different tones on the same basic sound. Nor are the lexical alternatives on the sound-plus-tone in any way related (how could they be and allow comprehension?).

The basic sounds of Mandarin are not hard to hear or repeat, and English speech-mechanisms can generally be quite well adapted to them. All syllables (and all words) end either in an open vowel or diphthong, or in the consonants -n or -ng. The sounds of Mandarin are soft rather than clipped or guttural, which should be remembered when studying them on a comparative basis as below.

Initial sounds needing special attention

The main difficulties here are best illustrated by contrasts between pairs of consonants. In English these differences are not significant – that is, they are small changes in the mechanics rather than in the meaning of sounds. In spoken Chinese, however, they are vital. The first group (four pairs) concerns the degree of aspiration.

p	as in 'pie'	The contrast to make is in the amount of breath released. To form
b	as in 'bun'	both these initials, press the lips together, then open them and allow air to rush out, without voicing either sound with the vocal cords. 'P' should be very breathy, 'b' not. Note that the *English* spelling concentrates more on voicedness than on aspiration.
t	as in 'tie'	Again English spelling does not reflect the real difference. Place the
d	as in 'dear'	tongue tip against the upper gum of the front teeth, withdraw it to release air plosively, not voicing either sound. 'T' is very breathy, 'd' less so.
k	as in 'cough'	A third pair of breathy/non-breathy initials. The back of the tongue is
g	as in 'gamble'	placed against the soft palate and withdrawn. The 'g' sound is particularly hard.
c	as in 'nu*ts*'	This pair is produced with the tongue tip loosely against the upper
z	as in 'a*dds*'	front gum, the breath rubbing through the gap thus formed. With 'c' plenty of breath, with 'z' little. Again the English brings in an extra voiced quality.

[25]

Note that the initials 'h' and 'f' are particularly breathy in Chinese.

h   as in 'loch'   but spoken very softly.
f   as in 'stuffy'

A second group (two pairs) involves contrasts in tongue-position. As the tongue is near to or distant from the palate, so the degree to which it influences the following vowel will vary (compare '*sie*nna' and '*s*end' for example).

zh	as in '*J*anuary'	The first is spoken with the tongue rolled slightly back-wards, as though pronouncing 'drum'. The second keeps the tongue-tip near to the back of the lower teeth, while raising the front of the tongue to the hard palate.
j	as in '*g*enuine'	
ch	as in '*ch*allenge'	The first sound is retroflex, the second palatal.
q	as in '*ch*ew'	

Lastly, three consonants which may give some difficulty unless a native Mandarin voice is available:

x	as in '*sie*sta'	Spoken rather thickly, palatal.
sh	as in '*sh*elter'	With lips drawn backwards, not rounded and pushed forward.

r   as in '*r*ent'   But with the vital difference that the lips are kept pulled backwards except where the following vowel is a round one. To produce this sound, make the 'sh' sound, vibrate the vocal cords, then change to 'r' while keeping the 'voiced' vibration.

Final sounds needing special attention

Regional vowel differences in spoken English make comparisons difficult without use of the International Phonetic Alphabet. The following equivalents based on 'southern English' pronunciation may, however, be useful.

a   between 'f*a*ther' and '*a*t'
an   'b*un*' rather than 'b*an*'
ang   'b*ung*' (no hard 'g' sound)
ai   '*ai*sle'
ao   '*ou*t'
e   between '*e*xit' and '*ear*th'
en   'rock'*n*'roll'
eng   'h*un*ger', with the 'u' flattened and no hard 'g' sound
ei   'l*ay*'
ou   's*ou*l' (never 'c*ow*')

i   'chlor*i*ne' (but after 'r', 's(h)', 'c', or 'z', this
       becomes an almost grunted 'eh', shorter and
       flatter than the sound that begins '*ear*th')
u   'z*u*lu'
ong   'J*ung*' (the Germanic 'u'-sound)
ian   '*yen*'
ui   '*way*'
ü   '*yew*'

Note that the above lists are not complete. They give
sound-comparisons for some elements only of Chinese
syllables, but do not define these or show how they
combine according to phonemic laws; thus 'zhe' exists
but not 'be', and 'bing' but not 'zhing'. The listed
sounds cover all those likely to give trouble, and should
be enough for the Chinese examples of later chapters to
be read in romanized form with fair accuracy.

On this basic sound-structure, the tones tend to
become relative to each other within the utterance
rather than stay absolutes. Thus, when two identical
syllables follow each other, as in *kànkàn*: 'to have a
look', and should theoretically both be spoken in the
fourth tone, what happens in actual speech is that the
second will be almost toneless and much lighter than
the first: kànkån. Often most of an entire sentence will
sound without tones, the voice choosing simply one or
two syllables to get full tonal value. When two or more
third tones coincide, only the final one of the series is
spoken as a full third tone, all earlier ones becoming

second unless the meaning demands that one receive particular emphasis. Relative also is the amount of 'fall' with the fourth tone, often taken for an emphatic (perhaps because a sharply falling cadence is usual in English with firm statements or commands?) but in fact quite without any such sense. The 'high' first tone is likewise easily pitched too high by the beginner. Indeed, in general when speaking at a reasonably fast speed a Chinese voice tends to find a given level and keep to it, reserving full tones for essential syllables. This level, once struck, will usually be held throughout an utterance with little cadence. This is particularly true with questions: these tend to stay on a high level throughout, unlike English ones with their varying cadence according to the answer expected. What the beginner should concentrate on, therefore, is the tone of essential syllables – indeed, he must do so if he is not to get completely inhibited from the outset – and he should listen hard to as much accurate spoken Chinese as possible in order to tune his ear to where the essential syllables generally come. It will reassure him to know that the margin for outright incomprehensibility from faulty tones is wide. Of course his speech will betray him as a foreigner; but his clothes would do as much.

If the tones are often skipped over, and if, even when fully sounded, they still do not necessarily hold a single immediately audible lexical meaning, then how does spoken Chinese make its meanings clear? One common way is by doubling-up into compounds: the single syllable takes a second syllable, both halves working towards a shared point rather as do the two arms of a triangle towards the apex. Thus, if in spoken English the sound 'home' were a homophone standing for much in addition to 'a dwelling-place', then for that prime meaning the compound 'homestead' could be used, and other compounds on 'home-' could be used for other senses. Chinese follows this pattern with its many homophones. It is not unusual to hear the question 'Do you mean "home" as in "homestead"?' if a listener is uncertain how he should understand a heard syllable. Modern written Chinese has been affected by this doubling-up process. It has less need for it, since the written character at once identifies tone, sound, *and* meaning; but none the less there are written compounds which probably originated from the need for spoken clarity, or from analogy with such a need.

Other ways exist in which Chinese sharpens its meanings. These raise questions touching on word-formation and grammar, subjects which are discussed in chapters 4 and 6 respectively. There is more general ground to clear first. The brief account of sound-structure given above will be enough for this to be followed, even though the student of spoken Chinese will want very much more on sounds.

First of the items to be clarified is the nature of Mandarin. The term, a non-Chinese one, suggests a language of class and authority. Or, like 'B.B.C. English' and 'East-Coast American', it might set up standards of accepted speech within a single language that has many regional dialects. There are indeed many dialects in Chinese, and it would be reasonable to take Mandarin for a refinement, concerned with orthodoxy and correctness much as is the Académie for French.

The truth lies in a historical accident, or rather in two such accidents. Modern Mandarin may be said to date from the Manchu overthrow of the Ming dynasty in 1644. The new rulers, a non-Chinese race, spoke many dialects among themselves and lacked a unifying language with which to rule. The variety of Chinese spoken in and around Peking was taken for this purpose, and because the new dynasty was strong, Mandarin quickly spread as 'official speech', that is, the speech of officialdom and of the court. It was not at first, nor was it intended to be, the speech of the people as a whole. But after the fall of the Manchus and the start of the Chinese Republic in 1912, it was necessary for the new China to have a national language and again the choice was Mandarin.

Historically and in linguistic origin, therefore, Mandarin is the speech dialect of the Peking region and nothing more. But this gives a false impression of the divisions of Chinese that are made by linguistic geography. To go by these, Mandarin is a separate language, differing from the languages of Shanghai or Canton in its sounds (less markedly in grammar) much as does Spanish from Italian or German from Dutch. Even among those who do speak Mandarin there are wide variations of accent, especially with Chinese who have learnt it as a second 'national' language in addition to their own local speech. The beginner will soon discover this when he tries out his phrases on a Mandarin speaker from (say) Shanghai. Fortunately, these variations are regular enough for the ear soon to adjust to them. It is these, the sub-lingual divergencies, which should properly be termed 'dialects' of Chinese. They are as far apart as is standard English when spoken in London and Yorkshire, in Washington and the Mid-West, and they will persist for such time as other regional varieties of Chinese continue to be spoken – which, put differently, will be for as long as Mandarin takes to become the national language throughout all China.

On this point estimates vary. One set of recent figures, which ignores the twelve million 'overseas Chinese', claims that the national language is today spoken by about 400 millions, given a minimum total of 560 millions who use Chinese of whatever form. The wording of the claim does not make clear whether what is meant is the national language as first, as second, or as only language, but progress in the last few years has been remarkable and the figure, however understood, is certainly on the increase.

'So if a Cantonese speaker in (shall we say) Hong Kong writes to a Mandarin-speaking friend in Peking, will the friend (and 400 millions like him) simply make different sounds in reading the letter aloud? And will all 560 millions of the Chinese linguistic community write the letter in the same way?' Yes – and no. Hong Kong as a centre of world trade is open to outside influences on language, such as Malay and Anglo-American. Its vocabulary is based partly on these, and partly on the variety of Cantonese adopted as *lingua franca* by local and non-local Chinese residents. A Hong Kong Cantonese-speaker will often write characters from the common stock of Chinese and give them a local meaning that does not stop their standard use in other contexts. If he is reporting local speech, the divergencies in his writing may be considerable. So the friend in Peking might be puzzled by the letter unless it had been written with care by an educated man. There are also of course many differences between Cantonese and Mandarin that reflect life rather than language.

It is nevertheless true to say that educated Chinese from whatever area have no problems of communication in writing, and few indeed in speech. A comparison of Chinese characters with our own Arabic numerals is often made, in that the numerals mean the same in (say) Poland and Italy despite the differing pronunciations they are read with, and that this also holds for the characters over all of China. At this point in the story, it is a true and useful comparison to make, though possibly one that implies greater vexations in *spoken* intercourse than in fact generally arise among the highly verbal and resourceful Chinese.

Script 2

A common belief about Chinese characters is that they are pictures written down back to front. This is quite wrong. But to examine the separate parts of this belief may be to clarify notions of Chinese script as something impossibly exotic and quaint, and to show that, though its forms are seemingly God-given since periodization of them along Western lines is an impossible (or at least an as yet scarcely attempted) task, there are certain lines of approach open to us.

In the first place, the rationale of Chinese writing has at least five separate elements. Pictorialism may be involved in all of these, just as sound-painting is involved in the phonetic scripts of the West. But to say that Chinese characters are all drawings of things or concepts is like saying that English words are all of the 'cuckoo' or 'rub-a-dub-drub' variety. Very few characters can today still be seen as pictures.

Secondly, taking 'written down back to front' to refer to the direction followed when writing a Chinese sentence, there is no absolute rule on this point. For the last decade, Peking has very wisely imposed 'left to right' horizontal lines as the form for both handwriting and printing. Elsewhere, and even in China among older people, the most usual handwriting direction is in downward columns, starting from the right margin. Overseas Chinese printing is less consistent. Very often the typographer seems to fix the direction of his lines only after he has made his overall page-layouts. This is particularly true of newspapers, which may run headlines left to right and right to left (horizontally) and right to left (vertically) on the same page, with the texts below them also varying (though a vertical direction is more common). Right to left horizontally, or 'backwards', is certainly out of fashion.

Thirdly, it is incorrect to say that the individual character is written backwards, that is, right to left in order of making the pen-strokes or component parts for it. This is never the sequence of single-part characters, and only rarely of characters with two or more parts. Left to right may be taken as the rule.

The notion of characters as pictures does, however, give an historical starting-point from which to approach the five different types into which they may be grouped. Certainly the earliest characters were pictures. Their first appearance on records of divinations (the so-called 'oracle bones' of about 1400 B.C.) shows a high proportion of recognizable drawings: ⊙ for 'sun' (now 日), 〗 for 'moon' (月). The number of drawings is greater at this date than when they appear several centuries later on bronzes of the Chou dynasty. But even as early as the oracle bones, the picture form was becoming bankrupt and other means were replacing it. Pictures could only serve for very concrete and widely familiar objects: 人 'man'(人), 牛 'cow'(牛), 川 'river'(川). Soon it was necessary to extend this pictorial basis into more abstract or symbolic areas. The extension cannot be dated, but quite early the swing towards symbolism had begun.

Examples of this second type include certain numbers (一 'one', with added strokes up to 三 'three'), basic modifiers (中 'middle', possibly an arrow 中 piercing its target 口, now written 中; 上(上) for 'above' and 下(下) for 'below', possibly the sun's position relative to earth), and a number of 'indicatives', in which an existing picture-character is given an added stroke drawing attention to a certain quality in it. The character 刀 'knife' when written 刃 means 'knife-edge'; 木 'tree' written 本 means 'root'. Or 'four grains of rice' 少 might be read as indicating a poor harvest, which would account for its present-day meaning of 'few, little'.

Characters of both these types are one-part and complete in themselves. The third type are the 'associatives' which rely for their meaning on the interaction or association of more than one part. 好 'good; to love' consists of the character 'woman' on the left and that for 'child' on the right, their combination leading naturally to the verb or quality directly associated with them. One can argue that the earlier 'four grains of rice' character belongs under this type, since it has to do with mental association; certainly the character for 'to tend' 牧 does, being composed of 'cow' 牛 plus 'hand and whip' 攴. With all these, an internal logic supplies the meaning. Other examples show routine pictures going over into abstract areas: 東 'east' is said to consist of 日 'sun' rising behind 木 'tree'. Two men one after the other 从 means 'to follow'. Many of the first characters learnt by the beginner are from this group, but the attractive etymologies that may be offered for them are not always to be believed. Often the explanations are traditional and may not stand up to recent linguistic research – which in the case of the oracle bones and bronzes is very recent indeed, dating as it does only from the turn of the century.

The fourth group of characters are the loaned characters, and these result from a process, seemingly inevitable, which has influenced the entire nature of the written language and its proliferation of separate script-items. As the stock of pictures and their derivatives became exhausted with the widening demands of language, so a sound with its own fixed character would lend this character to another similar sound lacking a written form. The two meanings were quite unalike. At first such loaning only took place where the two sounds were phonetically identical yet sufficiently far removed in sense and usage not to be confused. Thus, the character for 'peacock' was borrowed for 'sail', and that for 'growing grain' was borrowed for 'to come'. Loans of this type were already being made by the period of the Chou bronzes. In the modern language they are rarely seen or heard to be loans, due to changes in the script and in sound, but historical scholarship proves that they occurred as such. The principle behind them is important because it leads to the fifth, and most numerous, type of character.

This fifth group accounts for about nine-tenths of modern Chinese characters. In it, two or more parts are concerned. One part (often but by no means always on the right) is the phonetic or sounding element, while the other part is the specifier, which may have a bearing on the sense in which this phonetic is to be understood. Do not confuse the interaction here with that of the third associative type, which was of a logical kind in that both parts were equally operative in symbolizing a total meaning. The present type keeps its functions separate, one being to indicate, however vaguely, how the character is spoken, and the other to show what it means. An example is the character 防 'to guard against'. In this, the right part sounds, the left part specifies. With alteration of the specifier, the character can become 房 'house' (upper part specifying, lower part sounding), or 放 'to place' (left sounding, right specifying). The example is a good one, because the constant phonetic element (*fang*) is particularly strong and really does give an accurate indication of how to pronounce the various characters (and there are many more) which use it. (It is also good because the position of the specifier is seen to vary – now to left, now above, now to right – a factor which must be grasped early on.)

Unfortunately, the written language is only rarely so helpful with its sound-indications. There is, moreover, no link whatsoever between the phonetic as written and the tone in which the basic sound is spoken. As a clue to sound, the phonetic can at best only hint at the basic sound itself, and this leaves odds of 1:4 if guessing at the tone.

Some more examples of phonetic reliability: 痘 'small-pox' is made up of a phonetic 豆 written inside the specifier for 'diseases' 疒 . Here the phonetic element is completely reliable, since its own sound and tone are also that of the entire two-part character. With 河 'river', which consists of a phonetic 可 and the specifier for 'water' 氵 , the phonetic's clue to the whole character involves a change of consonant, as does that in the character 仙 'fairy' (pronounced slightly differently from its phonetic 山 which as a character in its own right means 'mountain'). Other phonetics diverge considerably from the pronunciation of entire characters in which they are found.

*

At this point there may well be questions requiring a closer look at the history of written Chinese. But since the chapter began with the notion of Chinese as pictures, it may be useful before going further to outline the conventions of drawing or writing in the language.

The Chinese often claim that the cultivation of a beautiful handwriting style is almost at one with painting, and hold it to be both a private discipline and a public display of the writer-artist's moral and spiritual worth. Do not be put off by this. Today there are probably no more real calligraphers in the Chinese world than there are real artists in the West. Most Chinese write as well or as badly as the rest of us, using a pencil or ballpoint pen and reserving the brush for more formal occasions.

Nevertheless, all Chinese writing is grounded in calligraphic forms. The script taught in primary schools (and used in this book) is the 'pattern style' followed more or less closely in typographic design, brush characters, neon signs, and indeed in any public or semi-public script. It would be wrong to compare this 'pattern style' with any Western copybook forms, since these usually teach a minimal basic shape, to be retained in adult handwriting. Chinese teaches an idealized script, with a maximal shape for each character, which is drilled until penmanship has become automatic and the character's outline is impressed onto the subconscious. Then the quicker handwriting of adulthood adopts the 'cursive' style, and drops or runs together many of the strokes while still suggesting the original ideal outline. 'Pattern style' is therefore correct but somewhat redundant. However, a foreigner, probably wishing to read printed Chinese for the most part, does best to keep to pattern style, which is closest to that of typography. No Chinese who may read his handwriting will judge it to be childish for that reason.

It was stated earlier that the 'left to right' rule applied in ordering the strokes or parts within a character. This may be put more precisely as 'top left point to lower right point'. The stroke is generally defined as the distance travelled by the pen in one direction without a lift from the paper, but this unit may be a curved line, a hook round an angle, or a straight line plus hook: the diagrams of chapter 10 explain this better than do words. Other rules, which may fill out or even replace the main one of 'left to right', are: top before bottom (e.g. where right-top is higher than left-top), left before right (where two strokes are level), outside before inside (but where an outside 'box' encloses inner strokes, the box is 'closed' below last of all), horizontal before vertical (in a single cross stroke), strokes slanted left before those slanted right, centre stroke before balancing strokes at the side. These rules are often ignored by Chinese themselves, however, and are meant only as a guide. The actual *direction* taken by the pen-nib while making a stroke is usually left to right; but again see chapter 10 for graphic illustration of this.

After a hundred or so characters have been fully studied, both stroke-order and pen-direction should begin to come naturally. The importance of both is of course that they contribute to the balance or 'rightness' of the written characters. In practical terms, however, this only affects writing in the cursive style, where the pen is seldom lifted from the paper as the character is formed. Were order and direction not correct, the pen would trace a different, probably meaningless outline. To test this, write any character in chapter 10 in haphazard order of strokes and without lifting the pen, and study the resulting shape against the correct one. Of all styles of Chinese writing, the cursive is thus paradoxically the most formal, since by reducing the number of strokes per character it limits the freedom of those that are written.

*

As we resume the historical account of the script, there should be two main questions on the information given thus far. First, if the term 'phonetic' is used in discussing the fifth type of character, then why is Chinese not a phonetic language? Second, if it is not, and has no alphabet, then how are its 'words' to be treated collectively, for example, in a dictionary or a technical account of linguistics?

The answer to both questions begins with the highly formative principle of loaning, which was noted as underlying the fourth and fifth group of characters. At the outset, these loans were only made between identical-sounding but meaningfully remote syllables. Soon it was necessary to give some further aid to understanding; for instance, the loaned 'peacock' character for 'sail' is written with a small square by it, to specify its new meaning. This formula of 'loan plus specifier' may be compared to the use of 'Jones the bread' in a Welsh village with many Joneses all needing to be distinguished from one another. At that period, unlike today, Chinese had too many sounds chasing too few characters. Use of the new formula was probably begun by some imaginative scribes early in the Chou dynasty (about 1000 B.C.), and it eventually went over into the fifth type of character that is so formative of the modern written vocabulary. But several stages intervened.

First of these was the loaning of characters for sounds that were almost identical but not quite. After this had started, not even the added specifier could ensure that the two sounds (one lending, the other borrowing a character) would later develop in exactly the same way. Thus, if the modern word 'Jones' had originally sounded something like 'jun' and had borrowed that sound's written symbol, the ancient 'jun' sound itself might have developed right away into (say) modern 'gin'. This does not matter in English, because such a divergence is visible in the symbol's spelling as well as in its sound: 'gin' is a different *word* from 'Jones'. In Chinese, on the other hand, the sounds diverged but their 'spelling' stayed the same. Loans which originally were near-twins would end with no audible relationship and yet the same outward appearance in writing. The result was the breakdown of what was very likely a truly phonetic language. For example, the sound *ta* ('much, many') in ancient Chinese seems to have lent its character (多) to several other sounds which later wrote in a specifier for their own individual meanings: 眵 'dim, watery' ('eye' specifier), 侈 'extravagant' ('man' specifier), 移 'to move, transport' ('grain' specifier). These at one time all sounded approximately *ta* (we know from old rhyming dictionaries). But in modern Chinese not one of them sounds anything like *ta*, and even the basic phonetic alone (多) in its own meaning of 'much' now sounds *duo*.

The use of the term 'phonetic' for fifth-type characters is thus correct historically but of doubtful merit otherwise. Modern Chinese characters hold few really firm clues as to their pronunciation. To state this another way, one has to know how they sound already before such clues can be judged useful or not. Today among Chinese, only those with specialist knowledge of philology have any idea how the early literature would have sounded at the time of its composition. Most people, if asked to read aloud an old poem, simply give the characters their modern pronunciation.

Philologists have other means to hand. They can reconstruct the sounds of ancient Chinese by going back to the old dictionaries. Influenced by Indian grammarians, early Chinese linguists tabulated their words by initial sounds on one axis and by finals on the other, and this valuable information is now available to philological research. (Even today some Chinese dictionaries, published for Chinese, follow the same method of sound-spelling.) However, the compilation and use of Chinese dictionaries, both old and new, generally involves the specifiers, and their special function must now be studied more closely.

When first introduced before the ninth century B.C., specifiers were labels of the simplest kind: 'hand' for graspable objects or for mechanical actions, 'mouth' for eating and speaking, and so on. Soon they began to operate with a reverse effect. A loan-character could with use become more established in its new sense than its old, and in such cases a specifier would be used with the original character to signify its earlier, pre-loan meaning. What did not alter was the function of the actual specifier. It might have a slightly transferred quality (as does 'Jones the bread' for 'Jones the baker'), but it still merely served as a rider to the phonetic loan.

About A.D. 100 work began on the *Shuo wen* dictionary, an analysis of a system of character-writing which had been promulgated centuries earlier by the emperor Ch'in. The *Shuo wen* recognized a total of 540 specifiers and adopted them as factors in classifying the characters. They stayed as a lexicographer's tool, sometimes varying in number, until the seventeenth century, when they were pruned to 214. These 214, since used for Korean and Japanese also, are better known as 'the radicals'. A dictionary lists them by the total of their component strokes, from 1 to 17, and enters in the dictionary the individual characters under each. The exact placing of any character under a particular radical is further governed by the number of strokes *extra* to the radical that go to make it up. This may sound clumsy as a system, but since there are seldom more than about twenty characters in any 'extra' sub-section, for the Chinese user it can be almost as quick to consult as an alphabetical ordering is for the Westerner.

Such, then, is the evolutionary end of the specifiers or radicals: a reference system, appropriate to any Chinese listing from a telephone directory to a dictionary. Radicals cannot be made to play any larger part in our task of getting at the meaning of Chinese characters – much less at the 'soul' of the language as is sometimes claimed. Unfortunately some Westerners cannot resist promoting this claim, often at the beginner's expense who welcomes eagerly any 'method' he may be offered. More profit could be had from a thorough study of phonetic development; but it is usually the radicals that are invoked, and it is worth seeing why they cannot do more for us than the Chinese themselves ask from them.

So far, the fifth-type character has been held up as a specifying element added to a phonetic, the two parts being quite separate in function. If this distinction had been kept, then the sound-development of the phonetic part (the story of 'Jones' and 'gin') would at least be the whole story, however complicated. But as we have seen, the specifiers consisted of highly important concretes, such as 'hand' and 'mouth', and not surprisingly these could be older than the phonetic loans they were put with. They could also have a strong phonetic identity of their own. Indeed, they could have begun as phonetics, only later becoming specifiers or radicals; the 'mountain' part of the character for 'fairy' (see page 39) is a phonetic in its use there, but can also elsewhere be a radical. Because of this strong sound, such specifiers could in turn be written with an added radical.

A considerable number of modern characters thus in effect consist of two radicals. One example of this is 請 *qǐng*: 'to ask'. Its right part is the 'green' radical *qīng*, here used only for sound-value, while the left part is the 'speech' radical *yán*, used to indicate meaning for the total character. Other characters will follow this use of *yán*, of course, but still others will use it on the right, phonetically: conversely, *qīng* will appear on the left, and as a radical. So the functions of phonetic and radical may be seen to alternate in one and the same element.

Another quite different source of confusion arose from the reduction of the radicals to 214 – a helpful measure but one which left behind a legacy of trouble. Nobody, as from one particular day in the seventeenth century, actually stopped *using* the characters concerned. They simply had to be re-classified, and successive dictionaries were obliged to fall in with the patterns then set. For example, the character for 'one hundred' (百 *bǎi*) belongs to the fifth character group, and has two radicals. The top part is the radical for 'one' (— *yī*), the lower part is the radical for 'white' (白 *bái*). At first glance, analysis seems straightforward: the lower part is surely the phonetic, since it matches the character's sound so well, while the upper part is the radical, 'one' being a significant item in 'one hundred'. In fact the character for 'one hundred' is listed under the 'white' radical in the dictionary. Such freaks of lexicography are by no means rare, and the Chinese themselves are often hard pressed to find a sought-for character.

Even without sound-developments, this would be enough. Include them with the above two sources of confusion, and all usefulness of the radicals as sense-indicators seems at an end. It is not quite as bad as that, but nevertheless the radicals are best treated by the beginner strictly as natural phenomena. Clues to the meanings of characters that they appear to offer should be followed up with caution. But just as certain phonetics have stronger sounds than others, so some radicals tend to stay meaningfully firm in the characters which take them. Among these are the radicals for 'metal' (the 'gold' radical), 'fire', 'bird', 'insect', 'knife', 'flesh', 'wind', 'water/liquids', and 'grass/plants'. But other radicals equally concrete will be found in widely extended characters that have nothing in common with such headings as 'silk', 'sun', 'heart', 'bamboo', or 'cowrie-shell' (=money).

What are worth learning at once, both as individual characters and as aids to using the dictionary, are those radicals which have lexical value by themselves, without the addition of a second part. Chapter 9 lists one hundred of them, as well as a number of compound expressions consisting solely of radicals. These, in terms of memory-storage, give two for the price of one.

It may also be thought worthwhile to learn the numbers (1 to 214), at least of the most frequently used radicals. Most Western-produced Chinese dictionaries carry a good deal of romanization in their sub-entries, and so are obliged to show in some way exactly which Chinese version of (say) *fa* or *fang* is in question; the radical number clarifies the point. The actual numbering of radicals, however, is a strictly Western procedure. No Chinese is likely to know that the 'fire' radical is No. 86, any more than a Westerner can say off-hand which letter of the alphabet is No. 20. All that the numbers do is make lighter the work of identifying characters and using dictionaries, and as soon as possible they should be dropped from the conscious memorizing process in favour of the total character's shape.

Reform: 1

It would be only natural at this point to ask why China has not long ago put its linguistic house in order. Even remembering that many of the problems of the last chapter concern our westernized approach to the language rather than the language itself, there is much inherent confusion that remains to trouble native and foreigner alike.

The truth is that for many centuries China has been trying to reform its written script. Even in the time of Confucius (sixth century B.C.), there were already so many arbitrary script variants as to cause the philosopher to complain. Things would always tend to get worse instead of better. Take the changes to phonetic elements discussed on pages 43–4, for example. These diverged not only with the passing of time but also with geographical distribution, related sounds in one dialect not necessarily paralleling those in another. The result was that, even if a liberally-minded dynasty might wish to implement a reform policy, it could not hope to carry this throughout the empire with equal force. Reforms to the script were thus undermined from the start by geographical and political factors – even given good intentions.

The first authorized reforms were made in the last years of the Ch'in dynasty (third century B.C.). A uniform method of forming characters, known as the 'small seal' style, began at this date, and the specifiers were brought under control. There were only a few thousand characters in existence. At least four centuries earlier, however, certain characters were already being given a more simplified form. For example 集, a character showing several birds perched on a tree, had come to be written 集 . Some of these very old simplifications are still in use today. Their number grew under the Han dynasty (roughly the start of the Christian era) along with the growth of cursive script. But at no time could this trend be said to be in the interests of a spread of literacy. A more likely motive for it was over-professionalism or sheer laziness on the scribes' part. The move towards simplification was never strong enough to counter the conservatism either of the language itself, with its need for more characters, or of the scholar-gentry anxious to preserve the *status quo* by which all office was theirs. Lexicographers made matters worse. Their dictionaries would include the complete stock of all known characters and expressions, plus variant forms, and not attempt to select or normalize; so that once a character had appeared in a dictionary, its pedigree was beyond question.

By the time of the Ming dynasty (fourteenth century)

a reaction against simplification had begun. Teachers would root out the shorter forms from their students' essays, for the imperial examiners failed candidates on sighting a single abbreviation. This mental attitude more than once led to China's missing a chance for reform inspired from outside. One such opportunity came with the Jesuit missionaries. They arrived in China at the end of the sixteenth century, having learnt fluent Chinese at their seaport headquarters of Macao with the help of romanization of the script. Their intellectual prestige at the Peking court was high. Chinese comments on the theory of romanization were favourable, but of course the Jesuit systems, intended for use by Westerners, could not be taken over wholesale by the Chinese, and the energy and insight needed to re-work them into a phonetic script suitable for native use was never found. Later, Protestant missionaries made great strides in teaching Chinese to natives of the coastal provinces via roman letters, and issued books and pamphlets in their script. Again the matter was shelved.

Two centuries later, the industrial revolution of the West seized on China's millions as a bottomless market for machine goods. The era of land grabs and unequal treaties forced the country towards a modernization which Japan was already undertaking voluntarily and with much success. Essential to this process were wireless telegraphy, the typewriter, modern printing, wider and more scientific education, all of which were badly handicapped by aspects of Chinese script such as we have already met. Japan had found an answer in her *kana* phonetic script, which was used alongside the ideographic characters (borrowed from Chinese) in writing. Again the advocates of language reform were heard, but not heeded, in China.

During the first Republic (1912 to 1949 on the mainland) much work was done towards a national language and a simpler script. Unfortunately most of this work stayed at committee-stage, where it was marred by considerations of nationalism, scholarship or personal prestige such as often attend sweeping measures of this nature wherever they are discussed. The many later attempts to implement method after method all eventually failed, whether through faults within the method, entrenched opposition to its advocates, or a simple lack of money and authority. There was not always agreement that Mandarin should be taken as the national language, nor even, once adopted, what its precise spoken form should be. There was also a good deal of confusion as to the aims of reform. Should they be to create a *new* Chinese? or merely to make learning the existing Chinese easier?

The *zhùyīn* (=phonetic) alphabet, for example, took some forty elements from standard character-forms and used them to show pronunciation. But as the normal Chinese form of the character was shown alongside for identification, this was only of value for teaching or reference work. Then again, the 'mass education movement' of the 1920s offered to teach illiterates on a basis of 1,000 characters. But were these characters seen as a stepping-stone to a larger vocabulary of (say) 5,000? Or were they to be a kind of 'basic Chinese' which would cover all normal written situations?

Such doubts extended to romanization schemes. In 1926 some leading experts put out a magnificent 'National Language Romanization' (or 'GR' – see chapter 12). This used internal changes of spelling to show the four tones of Mandarin, thus avoiding the marks used in this book and providing each sound-plus-tone with a different 'word'. It was and is the most accurate guide in roman letters to the national language, and so is of great value to foreigners. But it does not seem to have been intended to replace the characters for Chinese natives, even though there was speculation about how long it would take to eradicate them (one such guess said 1,000 years!). Certainly it never received full governmental backing. Perhaps its very accuracy would have worked against such a replacement: many educated Chinese, even if they are accustomed to looking at their language through a foreigner's eyes, find GR quite baffling in its spelling changes. Convinced of this fact, one British firm in Hong Kong planned to send its private cables in GR as a safeguard against industrial espionage, on the grounds that no Chinese would be able to intercept and read them. Eventually it was decided that unfortunately no Chinese cable-office would even be able to transmit such messages accurately.

A better illustration of the strength and the weakness of GR would be hard to find.

Despite such doubts and confusion, by 1930 it was clear that if Chinese were ever to become simpler to learn and to use, then a clean break, properly phased and financed, was essential. To a great many Chinese, some of them modernists and patriots, such a break was unthinkable. Even at that early date the matter had political overtones. A form of romanization known as 'Latinxua' was devised in the Soviet Union for resident Chinese and was later taken up in China, particularly in the areas under communist control, for both teaching and publishing. The Kuomintang government continued to teach characters. Promotion of the national language was one thing; to tamper with the traditions and culture of the country was another. Attitudes struck by both sides almost forty years ago have hardened. Today, Taiwan/Formosa, the home of the former Kuomintang since 1949, frowns on simplified Chinese and forbids the import of Peking literature not merely for political reasons but because of the associations of simplified script. The Peking regime, on the other hand, has followed its early course to the next logical stage. This, and its implications, must now be examined.

*

When talking about language reform simply in terms of wider literacy, one is tempted to see its advocates as heroes wrestling with reactionary dragons. In reality the whole question has formidable difficulties, and no answer to it can be a simple one – as is shown by the caution with which Peking, hardly behindhand in the struggle with reaction, now approaches the matter. Broadly speaking, the plan for reform is to standardize Mandarin as the national language throughout all of 'Han' China, that is, excluding the national minorities whose languages are not Chinese in origin and whose 'folk identity' is sacred in communist theology. To aid this, a modified form of Latinxua, renamed *pīnyīn* or 'phonetic spelling', was drawn up in 1956 and put to work in schools, also on street signs, railway trains and platforms, book jackets, and elsewhere, although it often accompanies the same legend in characters. *Pīnyīn* is the romanization used throughout this book (see chapter 12).

At the same time as declaring for Mandarin, with *pīnyīn* as catalyst in the experiment, the authorities approved a further plan which suggested that *pīnyīn* was designed eventually to become the written script itself. Early in 1956 the State Council in Peking ratified lists of 515 drastically simplified characters. These were not just isolated reductions but were obviously the first steps in an overall plan of simplification, for the first time in China's history promulgated officially. As it happened, more than half of the 515 were in general use already (some had been so for centuries), while other commonly-made simplifications at the same time were banned, thus making the net gain not immediately great. But the meaning of the plan could not be missed, backed as it was by some very thorough research (hundreds of reports were prepared) and by official and scholarly approval. More meaningful still was the announcement, since then repeated at intervals, that the new characters, like the old, will eventually disappear except as a medium for special linguistic or literary study. Simplification is therefore only to be temporary.

As might be expected, such a statement can only be made in guarded and non-committal terms. No time-limit can be set for the change to romanized script, nor are all Peking's comments in complete agreement as to its real probability. It is hard to imagine a change to *pīnyīn* occurring before the end of the century for anything but the most routine areas of language. Simplified characters will surely continue to be used for at least another generation *after* the final establishment of Mandarin as the national, and first, language. Theoretically, however, there are no valid objections to *pīnyīn* as a general script (the old fear that it will not distinguish strings of near-identical monosyllables has long ago been killed: the Chinese simply do not speak in strings of monosyllables, near-identical or otherwise). But some practical doubts remain.

One such concerns the persistence of ideographic links. Traditional written script is often praised as the great unifying factor that enables all Chinese from whatever province to communicate, no matter which variety of Chinese they speak. In one vital respect, however, it may be said to work against unity. A literate man from (say) Fukien province will see each character in his vocabulary with an almost ineradicable mental sound associated with it. As a child he learnt his characters to fit the sounds of his local speech; as a man, it will be asking too much of him to learn them a second time, in relation to Mandarin. While characters still exist, whether traditional or simplified, with *pīnyīn* or without, he will automatically read them as sounds. His children are likely to keep these sound-links to some extent, even though they may be taught Mandarin in the classroom. All this will delay the effective introduction of *pīnyīn*, since this can only occur when Mandarin sound-associations are total.

A second practical need will be for close parity of style in speaking and writing. Anything that may be spoken in Chinese may also be transcribed into *pīnyīn* and read back intelligibly. But this does not mean that the Chinese will continue to *write* as they speak. If styles diverge too far, there may well be a danger of separating out, despite all Peking's efforts to ensure that intelligentsia and peasants have a common vocabulary. Chapter 5 looks more closely at this point.

One more cause for concern is often quoted by the anti-reformists as a clinching argument against *pīnyīn*. It serves to introduce another quality of the ideographic script avoided until now.

What was said on pages 23 and 30 gave the impression that the meeting-place of sound, tone, and single lexical meaning is in the character, which can only sound in one way and only stand for one immutable idea. This is only partly true. Chinese characters have always been capable of attracting new meanings. (It has already been noted that occasionally a specifier would be used to fix a loaned character *back* into its original sense.) There are wide shades of meaning for many characters with a fixed sound and tone, and these depend on context. 方 *fāng* is one of these. Its prime meaning is 'square', but this is soon extended, first to cover related things such as a crossing or cardinal point in architecture, but later to very distant notions such as Taoist magic. All these uses are given the same *fāng* sound. Other characters, however, may signal the change in meaning by a change in tone. For example, 種 *zhong* in the fourth tone means 'to plant', but the same character given a third tone reading means 'seed, kind, sort'. Yet more characters have two entirely different basic sounds for meanings that have nothing in common: 還 may be read either as *hái*, meaning 'still, yet', or as *huán*, meaning 'to return, give back'. Context alone makes these senses clear.

The older Chinese literature relies heavily on this very ambiguity among identical characters. How is it then to be transmitted in *pīnyīn* to the millions of new readers who may not know characters? Before a character can be written in phonetic script and given a tone, it must first be interpreted or glossed as having one fixed sense.

The blurred outlines of ideographic script, with its several possible senses made even less distinct by the passing of centuries, must thus be made sharp enough to be lexically unambiguous. Even if this is possible, will the result still be Chinese literature? And if the old literature is made the exclusive property of scholars and sinologists, as Peking suggests, will this not shut it off from the non-specialists? It is hard to imagine otherwise. Yet the communists will not lightly throw over their literary past, for no previous republic or dynasty has promoted and reinterpreted it with such enthusiasm (huge editions of 'approved' classics are issued, some in simplified characters).

Another argument against *pīnyīn* as a medium for the old literature concerns style rather than characters and so belongs in chapter 5, which deals with reforms of style. What the foreigner has to decide about the whole question of simplified characters and *pīnyīn* is: whether he wants them. There are arguments for keeping to traditional script which is still used throughout the overseas Chinese world. One may read for a degree in Chinese at a Western university without departing from it. Probably no printing firm outside mainland China has a fount of the new characters, whereas millions of books exist in the old.

One way to approach the subject is to decide what kind of reading will be done initially (communist or non-communist), and then to learn the characters appropriate to it. The experience behind this advice is that after a first few hundred have been learnt, the characters for a time become hard to retain. To be faced at this stage with a double task – first the traditional forms and then the simplifications (or vice versa) – might daunt even the stoutest heart. Later, after about 1,000 have been learnt and certain recurring conventions have implanted themselves in his memory, the student will probably find that the learning process has become much easier, and that he can switch from one type of script to the other, filling out the gaps in his knowledge and mastering both scripts.

Words 4

We have seen something of how characters are formed and of what happens when ways to do without them are put forward. It will already be clear that one character equals one syllable; the purpose now is to show that one syllable, whether spoken or written, is not necessarily a word.

Some such demonstration may already have seemed called for by earlier pages, where even a casual glance at the romanized characters will have noticed them appearing in groups of two or more syllables and looking very much like words. If romanization is a Western invention, then who draws up the rules for grouping these *Chinese* syllables? What indeed makes a Chinese word, and how do the units of language relate to each other? Is the relationship that of English? Does it matter?

A few general terms from linguistics are needed at this point. First, a 'word' is usually defined as 'the minimum free form consisting of one or more morphemes'. A morpheme is the smallest formal or meaningful unit of language, that is to say, 'bread' has one morpheme, as has 'treacle', whereas 'badly' has two morphemes. A free form is one or more syllables that may stand alone with meaning (as distinct from a bound form such as the '-ly' in 'badly'), and a free form may itself be made up of free syllables, for example the word 'breadboard'.

On the printed page, each character of Chinese has as much right as any other to be taken for a word: adjacent characters are equally spaced apart and no functional clusters appear to be marked off. Furthermore, changes to the character itself, such as in English would make the letter 'l' into a 't' or the word 'pine' into 'pin', do not happen with any such effect. The key to the nature of a Chinese word lies in grasping a quite different and for the Westerner quite new correspondence between speech and script. In terms of raw material, the syllabic apparatus is the same as ours: syllables are either 'full' (that is, with lexical meaning) or 'formal' (contributing mechanically to grammar or syntax) or 'empty' (which means interjections, exclamations, and other physiological disturbances). The difference starts with the use made of this apparatus. Chinese is not concerned with writing sounds phonologically, but instead is concerned with morphemes; and, of the three types of syllable, it can only authentically transcribe the first two: thus it is a formal and lexical system of writing. Phonological systems of course quite often write their homophones differently – as does English with 'write' and 'right' – to bring out a formal or lexical change of importance, but Chinese always spells by form and function and all its homophones have these written differences. This means

[63]

that almost every individual character can be a morpheme.

But the special nature of written Chinese does not affect matters concerning the spoken-syllable-to-word relationship. A Chinese character is always one spoken syllable, and that syllable often on its own a 'free' word, but the language's words are not inevitably monosyllables and neither would a staccato series of 'full' syllables necessarily make sense when spoken aloud. Relationships between syllables, their closeness and freedom, and the balance of lexical to formal elements are as important in Chinese as in any other language.

English is often held up as 'analytic', that is, built mainly of free forms grouping into free words. Earlier in its history it was more 'synthetic' and had more bound syllables, so that the predominance in it now of free elements may be recent and perhaps impermanent. Chinese is also analytic: its words are often reducible to syllables which can on their own form words. Thus, two free syllables, separately meaning 'fire' and 'carriage', combine in *huǒchē*: 'railway train', a 'typical' Chinese word of two morphemes. But we must look further before deciding whether the analytical label is entirely right and whether the typical will remain so for all time.

Looked at for function, the quality of Chinese syllables which stands out at once is their aversion to becoming ranked in permanent hierarchies. The various English ways of enlargement of the root by affixed derivatives (the '-or' of 'doctor', for example) are hardly found in Chinese, and never with the closeness and predictability of a series like 'through-throughout' going over via accent-shift into 'thorough-thoroughly-thoroughfare'. A lexically more related series such as 'fish-fisher-fisheries' would of course be translatable into a similar Chinese series, in so far as the sound meaning 'fish' would be heard at each point, but in functional terms there is none of the English warp-and-woof closeness between the Chinese stages. And this lack of inherent ranking is borne out by the even more obvious absence of formal syllables to be inflected by grammatical change at the end of words.

Until quite modern times it was usual to regard a language of this uninflected kind as primitive compared to the scientific languages of Indo-European descent. Lack of inflectedness is today seen as a highly sophisticated linguistic quality. It calls for an elaborate frame of reference implying a common culture shared by speaker and audience, and in general uses very flexibly such grammatical means as do exist in the language. All this is true of Chinese.

The sophistication clearly emerges from the ease with which Chinese syllables coalesce into spoken words while rejecting labels as fixed parts of speech. A free monosyllable may indeed form a word in itself, but there are pressures always on it to enlarge and attract other syllables, free or bound. Chapter 1 introduced the simplest of these groupings in the doubled-up compound *kànkàn*: 'to have a look'. There are then a number of conventional word-forming syllables which start life by being full but become formal when added to others: noun-suffix examples are *zǐ* (basic full meaning: 'son') and *tóu* (full meaning: 'head'). These act somewhat like an anchor to other syllables. Thus, the spoken syllable *jiàn*, meaning 'shuttlecock', as heard and out of context, may have several additional meanings. When it is suffixed by -*zǐ* and become *jiànzi*, the meaning of 'shuttlecock' is more firmly pinned, for the only other *jiànzi* meanings are 'piano key' and 'bolt lock' and these are hardly likely to cause confusion. A similar anchoring is effected by -*tóu*, usually with a firmer and less generalized result; thus *zhōngtou*, literally 'clock' plus -*tóu*, has the meaning of 'hour'. Used in this way, *zi* and *tou* change into formal syllables, pronounced with almost no speech-accent.

Both *jiànzi* and *zhōngtou* are groups suffixed with one bound syllable, and form two morphemes. Two free syllables were seen above to form the two morphemes of *huǒchē*. Then there are syllables which are always bound, such as *gōng*: 'public', which exists only in conjunction with other syllables, as in *gōngyúan*: 'public park', again two morphemes. But bound forms of this kind are quite different from those found in the great number of compounds which depend on lexical repetition. An example of such is *yǔyán*: 'language', where both *yǔ* and *yán* are meaningful units, both separately with the idea of 'language' but never found as free

forms. Other compounds with bound forms are themselves 'bound', in that they are used only in conjunction
with other words or elements. Here an example is the
compound *zhōnghuá*: 'Chinese', which has two bound
syllables, one with the literal meaning of 'Chinese' and
the other with a figurative extension for it; this compound
adjective is always bound to its noun (e.g. *yǔyán*). Both
zhōnghuá and *yǔyán* have two morphemes each.

So the words of Chinese are by no means all monosyllables. Indeed, not even all its morphemes are: there
is a small group of two-syllable words (further to the
yǔyán type) which form single morphemes, neither half
having any meaning or function without the other. One
such is *pútáo*: 'grape', as much a polysyllabic morpheme
as the English 'treacle'.

At this point we may try to pin down an intrinsic
difference between English and Chinese syllable-to-word
relations, at cost to two hallowed beliefs. First to go is
the idea that Chinese is in any sense a monosyllabic
language, even though it is written down in characters
which are usually single morphemes. The second belief
to be discarded is that which would have Chinese and
English as analytic languages in the same way and in
the same direction (a query was left after this on page
64). English began as a synthetic language and became
less so as its free forms increased. Chinese certainly was
and is recognizably analytic, but as the number of its
bound syllables and compounds seems currently to be
growing, so the language must in time become more

synthetic, and this – if one may with any profit compare the direction in which languages move – means that Chinese and English are developing in opposite ways. The confusion as to how romanized groups of syllables should be joined up is a reflection of this fact.

To summarize: Chinese has few syllables bound as completely as *pútáo*: 'grape' (both of which are bound, and to each other) or *bócài*: 'spinach' (the first of which is never found away from the second), but many morphemes like those of *yǔyán*, loosely bound and capable of joining with other morphemes although never appearing as free words. Recent usage in mainland China also favours formal derivatives (earlier noted as rare), which increase the number of compound words. So most syllables and syllabic groups in modern spoken Chinese are best seen as loosely related to their fellows. It is not the purpose here to examine this relationship more closely – were it so, lengthy qualifications of 'free' and 'bound' would have to be made. But it should now be clear that spoken Chinese, seldom polysyllabic in the way it forms its morphemes, is entirely so in the way it joins them up.

*

Western influence on the vocabulary of Chinese is always a good barometer of prevailing social and political conditions within the country. The Han period (roughly that of the early Christian era) was a time of many word-loans which came in via the Central Asian trade routes, while the success of Buddhism by the fourth century brought still more. Manchu influence began with their dynasty in the seventeenth century, when the new rulers from the north added their non-Chinese expressions first of all to the speech of the imperial court and later, through osmosis, to the vocabulary of the common people. But none of these sources was as formative as was the invasion of China by nineteenth-century Western commerce and mass communications. To begin with, the new terms were translated phonetically: *démókèlāxī* for 'democracy', *sīdíkè* for the totally new concept of a walking-stick. Then came a form of translation by halves, one phonetic and one lexical, as in *fàlānróng*, which breaks down into '*fàlān*-felt', or the English-made flannel cloth. During this era there were even a few happy inventions whereby both the English and Chinese sound were made to coincide with sense: *yōumò* for 'humour' is one. A more essentially Chinese method than any of these was to give an equivalent to the idea behind the new word. By this, 'democracy' became *mínzhǔ* or 'people-rule' and 'walking-stick' became *shǒuzhàng* or 'hand-pole' with reasonable fidelity to both languages. The process often occurred via Japanese, an oriental bridging medium already much Westernized which could make the borrowings more natural and acceptable for Chinese. Terms such as *mùdì*: 'purpose', *zònghé*: 'synthetic', *fǒudìng*: 'negation', and *fúwù*: 'service' are loans to Chinese from Japanese constructs.

Widespread though this borrowing was, Chinese vocabulary remained in essence much the same at the turn of the century. In any language, alien grafts are apt to be rejected by the existing stock of native roots unless they are enforced by politics or conquest, as were Norman French grafts onto English. China has never known a lasting political domination of this kind. When conquerors have come, it has been they who have had to adopt Chinese ways (and particularly the language) in order to rule. But now, as China enters the technological age in the second half of the twentieth century, her linguistic position is critical and she seems obliged consciously to make large-scale grafts or adaptations for the first time in her history. In the area of modern scientific terms, the language is well suited to those of general meaning, less so to specifics or abstracts. There is a fondness for description as against mere labelling. For example, the magnetic compass (a Chinese invention) is the 'point-south-needle'. Modern chemical terms are more formal, and replace the dog-Latin syllables of Western scientific language ('per-', '-ate' and '-ide') with their rough equivalents in *gùo*, *sūan* and *huà*, using appropriate radicals such as those for 'stone' or 'metal' or 'gas' when writing chemical elements in formulae. Physics can manage more elegantly, while the human sciences generally read better in Chinese than in Western languages: 'sphygmomanometer' is not a lovely word, but its Chinese equivalent, the three characters for 'blood-pressure-calculator', is clear at once.

Yet as an illustration it does underline the dilemma of modern Chinese. Can the language continue for much longer to walk the tightrope between foreign terms borrowed for sound-value alone, and those given a descriptive or pictorial equivalent using traditional means of word-formation?

*

This chapter has discussed the morphology and the nature of words with one aim only: to emphasize that a Chinese word need not be a monosyllable, nor a monosyllable a Chinese word, and that the script is more immediately meaningful than is the spoken syllable. This is vital to what follows. If the point has been fully grasped, then the next chapter can move on to see how this affects style and literacy.

Reform: 2

We have seen already how China's language reforms should not be viewed in too heroic a light. 'Reform' is a loaded term. Its use in this chapter covers a change in the relation of written to spoken Chinese, and may suggest that the earlier style shared certain qualities (now 'improved') with some entirely satisfactory way now in use. This is by no means true beyond all argument. Indeed, it is ultimately the question of this sharing of qualities, rather than any actual reforming, that is the real point.

Linguistically speaking, Mandarin is a regional speech dialect. From the time of its adoption as the national language, however, it has always been linked with the idea of national literacy. A social problem needing a practical answer, this cannot simply lie in more characters for all.

For thousands of years, the main obstacle to social progress in China was the gulf between common speech (as spoken by gentry and peasants alike) and literary usage. From about the twelfth century, some literature (mainly novels and operas) was written in the vernacular, and much earlier this style had been the medium for private writings such as letters and poems. The true scholar despised these products, or had to pretend to do so when the official style was required. There is no evidence that the literati deliberately maintained this gulf as a means of class protection; but it amounted to that. No 'movement to the people', such as occurred in nineteenth-century Russia, could take place until there was a language for writing which could be understood by people who had no education in the classics and wanted simply to write. Furthermore, there was not much to be gained from an increase in literacy without suitable published material available for the newly literate in the characters they had been taught. Not until the end of World War I did a 'literary revolution' call for a return to the example of the vernacular novel, encouraging the use of 'spoken language' (*bái huà*) for these written ends. And even this call arose from literary rather than from social dissatisfactions.

The literary language (*wén yán*) has always tended to express one idea with one character, rather than with the compounds of more than one syllable which were looked at in chapter 4. Some scholars claim that in this it reflects the structure of ancient Chinese speech, which also avoided polysyllabic clusters. This may be so, but in more recent times speech has certainly evolved from isolated unsignalled syllables. *Wén yán* has not. Since it is understood by the eye and not the ear, it has not needed to distinguish the numerous homophones that keep speech always close to ambiguity. Confronted by a literary passage, a Chinese reading it aloud is able to follow its sense far more easily than is his audience. What usually happens, therefore, is that such a reader will add to and amplify his text so as to make its meaning clear without actually changing the substance as this emerges in spoken form. Naturally, some passages from the classics are too sacred for such treatment, and are learnt and recited in a manner almost unintelligible to the ear. But still today *wén yán* continues to be practised and its effects to be observed.

There are, admittedly, some practical advantages in this situation. Official instructions, street-signs, formal inscriptions, and artistic writing all benefit from the terse economy of *wén yán* with its 'one idea, one character' structure. A well-composed piece of literary Chinese yields up its sense more quickly than would the same ideas in spoken or written *bái huà*, or in translation into a foreign language. But in other ways the style is totally unsuited to modern life. Lawyers trying to draft internationally valid agreements have found literary Chinese, so clear on its home ground, quite inadequate for watertight phraseology capable of holding up under the pressure of challenge. Translators of political or economic ideas needed by modern China also met with difficulties; tradition demanded the high literary style, as in memorials to the emperor, but accuracy rejected it, even though many of the new coinings themselves were equally poor. Pressures and tensions continue to this day; a style of writing which veers between *wén yán* and *bái huà*, often taking the worst of both, will amuse and distress Chinese with a feeling for their language.

The Republican government, willing to look into all kinds of language reform, never fully met the challenge at the stylistic level. Efforts to teach 'basic Chinese' got nowhere, because nothing appeared that was printed in it. Even newspapers continued to be written in a kind of telegraphese that relied heavily on reference of one kind or another (overseas newspapers continue to appear in this style). This telegraph style is almost another language, and has its own special rules for abbreviation.

It was the communists who really backed the idea of a popular written idiom. They took up the *bái huà* of the older 'literary revolutionists', renaming it *pǔtōnghuà* or 'common speech'. The inspiration became firmly social. *Pǔtōnghuà* is now what the West generally thinks it means when it speaks of 'Mandarin' – in the sense of being the kind of Chinese that is most widely used and understood. It is adopted by all the communications media in China in its purely spoken form (the phrase 'national language' is not heard), while in print it is virtually standard in all publications except for specialist research journals or editions of ancient texts.

A new question arises with this idiom: how to keep *pǔtōnghuà* the same in both its written and its spoken form – and, given success in so doing, how to avoid certain bad side-effects. This problem was mentioned on page 58, as it affected *pīnyīn* or alphabetic writing (not surprisingly, since *pīnyīn* must stand or fall by the vernacular). Although the characters and even many of the phrases of *wén yán* are still used today, the 'literary style' itself is officially no more. Two factors suggest that a new such style must eventually emerge. First, it is not possible to equate politics with linguistics. The Chinese communists reached power through a peasant-based revolution, and the peasant is still the theoretical and practical target of propaganda. Party leaders, from Chairman Mao downwards, have shown in their writings and speeches that they fully understand this. But not all writing can be propaganda of or for the peasantry. The simplest spoken language tends to find a more elevated tone of voice when its ideas are written, even though the intended public is the same; thus Western tabloid newspapers use a vocabulary far removed from that spoken by their readership. Good communists may therefore continue to be one with the masses in their speech, but can hardly remain so in their writing until a colossal educational transformation has occurred. The second factor making for a new literary style is the persistence of abbreviation in Chinese. This again is a result of sound-poverty. When a language has only a few distinct units of sound, these have to do more work than they would if there were more of them, just as a short pump-handle takes greater effort to operate than a long one. In writing down ideas it takes no great sophistication to seek ways of compressing them in order to save oneself trouble; even phonetically rich languages encourage this process, so it can hardly be prevented with written Chinese.

What of the side-effects from the standardization of *pǔtōnghuà* in writing? These concern sentence-types, or grammar, due for consideration in the next chapter, but briefly stated they are that certain patterns will become almost as capable of misunderstanding as would spoken *wén yán*, though for opposite reasons. These patterns recur with something of the frequency of the homophones, because Chinese parts of speech lack formal labels and tend to need constant reiteration of their function in a sentence. Already today, only a few years after the acceptance of *pǔtōnghuà*, a leading article in the Peking *People's Daily* may seem verbose and heavy in its efforts to stay 'spoken'. Another side-effect may be a period of uncertainty as to what exactly 'good Chinese' is. For as long as the classics continue to be held in esteem in China there will be tensions between the old and new 'good styles', the more so since many educated Chinese are prone to inject literary tags into conversation, as Chairman Mao's own speeches show.

For the foreigner learning both to read and to speak, all this may seem irrelevant. Not for him to worry about what is or is not good style; all he wants is to know what it means, and how to use the characters himself. This is precisely why he must know something of these matters concerning appropriateness of style. To learn at random phrases or characters and use them indiscriminately is to risk seeing a Chinese face turn completely blank. But what selective filter can he apply as he is learning?

First, characters which belong more or less exclusively to *wén yán* and are very rarely spoken must be kept on a different page of the word-list, or somehow earmarked. Secondly, among the great bulk of phrases, sounds and characters that will remain after this first sorting, those learnt by hearing and those met in a piece of modern writing must be kept in two separate bundles until there is evidence that they can come together again. *Pǔtōnghuà* is already beginning to separate its functions, and much of it is not likely to be met off the printed page. (The student of reading alone is better placed. He may have a limited vocabulary centering round a special field of interest, but it would at least be a stable vocabulary.) Thirdly, if classical Chinese is being studied alongside modern, the student should keep separate notebooks on each style in all its aspects: syntax, vocabulary, idiom. An all-purpose approach may end in having no purpose.

Fourthly, some assessment is needed of the 'four-character phrases' (*chéngyǔ*) that will frequently be met, that is, of which can be spoken and which not. Many are from *wén yán*, however 'oral' their English translation may seem, e.g. 水滴石穿 *shuǐ dī shí chuān*: 'water wears away a stone', or 井底之蛙 *jǐng dǐ zhī wā*: 'judge the world from one's own backyard'.

If working with a native Chinese, the student should

spend a few minutes of each lesson (after about the first six months) on checking as to whether characters or phrases met with may be spoken, written only, or both. This becomes more important, not less, with progress. The native teacher may be reluctant to commit himself when this check is made, but it is vital that he do so if the student is to build up confidence of being understood.

Lastly, a warning about *wén yán* which applies if the language is studied in an overseas Chinese community. Chinese films are a most useful adjunct of study, but their character-titles seldom match the dialogue, *wén yán* abbreviations being very common. Sometimes these are acceptable in speech (such as *jīn* for *jīntian*, *shí* for *shíhou*, etc.), but the more recondite of them might be misapplied. So most attention should be given to the sounds of dialogue, unrelated to any titles – which anyway will probably flash past too quickly for the beginner, audience perception-rates for ideographs being in general higher than for roman letters.

Functions 6

'Don't waste time talking about Chinese when you should be talking Chinese' is excellent advice. The best way to learn a language is to live in the foreign community until its basic sentence-structures are automatic to one's thinking. If this is impossible, then these conditions should be imitated from abroad, especially when learning Chinese since little can be said about it in English easily. Thus the twelve sections of this chapter, each of which discusses a different functional aspect of Chinese while keeping to English terms, must make apology for going against this advice.

The first point to establish is that analysis of basic Chinese structures on their own would imply an already firm decision to learn the language. Analysis of Chinese into its immediate constituents (whereby the language writes its own grammar) is a process needing acquisitive, step-by-step comprehension. In effect, it is *the work of learning Chinese*; the task can only be shorter if one is already at home with formal linguistic techniques. However, many readers of this chapter will not yet be sure whether or not to learn Chinese. All they will know is that they would like to look into its functions and syntax. For them – and for those already studying who have hit problems – the viewpoint must be from English, and the statements made about Chinese must make sense now rather than in retrospect.

The second reason for this approach must be spelt out carefully. Just as study of the Chinese characters may show that Western phonological scripts are not the only means of human communication, so a comparison of grammar and syntax may lead to similar insights on that front also. Almost anything that can be said in English can be said equally well in Chinese, yet the various items of this chapter may at times seem to imply the opposite, dealing as they do with functional efficiency on a basis of comparisons. However, comparative linguistics is not a prize-giving ceremony. If we have become Eurocentric in this matter or in others, then it should not encourage the thought that things European are of themselves better; we cannot know this until we have looked beyond Europe. Comparisons may help us to judge wisely.

*

Number

Western languages show number in some structural or inflected way, that is, by changing the singular word. Sometimes number is seen in the noun, sometimes in the verb, but not always regularly in either (the English 'you go' is both singular and plural). A function of language is to define, however inconsistently, the quantity of things under discussion.

Chinese does not share this concern. There are no internal vowel-changes in nouns, such as make 'goose' into 'geese'. Secondly, verbs and adjectives do not vary with number. Thirdly, there are no inflected suffixes to show plural with a great many different kinds of nouns (as in English) or nouns and their adjectives (as in French, German and Italian for example).

The script also ignores number. In ancient Chinese, a character written as 'four fishes' stood for 'to fish'; similarly today the character made up of 'three trees' 森 does not mean 'trees', a plurality of 'one tree', but 'dense, thick'; and the 'three men' character* 众 [眾] only means 'many, all' when compounded with another character giving the idea of people *en masse*. Written Chinese does have a 'ditto' sign, but it is simply a shorthand device, not a pluralizer. Script repetitions are common enough, but they indicate a different type of word, not a different number of the repeated item.

One noun-suffix exists, 们 [們] -*men*, used with the personal pronouns 'we', 'you' and 'they' and with people who have some shared quality: 'my friends', 'the workers', 'his colleagues'. It is not used when a numeral is present.

As plural is formally the same as singular, the concept of agreement between noun and verb number does not

* In this chapter, characters are first given as simplified, with the 'regular' form in brackets.

apply. 有 人 来 [來] *yǒu rén lái*: 'have-person-come' may mean 'a/the person(s) has/have come', or simply 'someone's come'. This ambiguity and terseness accounts for much of the language's flavour.

Aside from pure numerals (see *Pre-statements*) there obviously must be ways of specifying a plural noun. Most frequent of these is 都 *dōu*: 'all', used after the noun qualified: 他 们 [們] 都 来 [來] *tāmen dōu lái*: 'they are all coming'. It is more flexible than the English translation 'all' might suggest – indeed, 'all' should be avoided except for the positive, inclusive sense. (If used with a negative verb, the meaning is 'none of': 他 们 [們] 都 不 来 [來] *tāmen dōu bùlái*: 'none of them is coming', and it has other uses as an adverb meaning 'entirely'.) *Dōu*, indeed, is a characteristic word in having a firm meaning only when related to other parts of the sentence.

Another specific pluralizer is 些 -*xie*, forming part of the indicators 'these' (这 [這] 些 *zhèixie*), 'those' (那 些 *nèixie*), and 'which?' (哪 些 *něixie?*), also 'some' (有 些 *yǒuxie*) and 'a good deal' (好 些 *hǎoxie*) used pronominally: 'of the men who have come, some are my friends'.

These are the only formal ways of marking a plural. The effects of this shortage are seen (page 87) in the use of numbers and measure-words, but the neutral, open nouns and verbs are part of the fibre of the language and cannot be criticized for ambiguity unless this is acknowledged.

Perhaps Western languages may indeed be faulted for overmuch attention to number. When philosophizing about mankind, or otherwise making what could be personal remarks in a non-personal sense, Chinese does very well. The existence of a single invariable idea for 人 *rén*: 'man', for example, makes generalizations less dangerous than do our own portentous labels ('Man', 'l'homme'), which invite challenging questions if – as is most usual – they are not meant literally. The Chinese *rén* is demonstrative or general, singular or plural, personal or all-inclusive, abstract or concrete, as the viewpoint on the matter in hand asks it to be.

Verbal attributes

The Chinese verb does not conjugate and has no tenses or moods. Formally only its willingness to take the negative prefix 不 *bu-* distinguishes it from a noun. But 'adjectives' may also take a negative; so clearly, as parts of speech, verbs and adjectives to some degree overlap. The ground they share is a useful basis from which to begin analysis in greater detail.

Two verbal groups exist, one covering verbs of doing, making, moving, etc. – the usual Western 'active' verbs with all auxiliaries and co-verbs. The other group is of states of being: 紅 (红) *hóng*: 'red', 好 *hǎo*: 'good', 漂亮 *piàoliang*: 'beautiful'. These in Chinese are not merely attributes given to a noun, but subjective verbal conditions. In saying 'The flower is red' (花 紅 (红)

hūa hóng), Chinese makes no translation of 'to be'. The idea of 'redness' is well enough linked to 'flower' by *hóng* alone. A sentence *hūa shì hóng* (是 *shì* = 'to be') would be possible only as confirmation of the flower's redness after this had been questioned: 'The flower *is* red'. But 'red' as simple adjective, as meaning 'redness', and as the verb 'to redden' is all contained in *hóng*.

With this verbal adjective in mind, Ezra Pound and others have reasoned that Chinese is more direct, more 'imagist' in its view of natural qualities than are other languages. A more critical judgement is that its lack of clear word-functions (here, the verb-adjective overlap) could make Chinese a poor medium for logical and philosophical ideas, where categories of expression may be as important as what is expressed. Neither attitude takes enough account of social-psychological factors, however, and these – fashionably termed 'structuralism' – can illuminate a language from within at no outlay of praise or blame for its superficial qualities.

Technically the two verb-groups have some points in common. Both can be used as predicates: 狗 跑 *gǒu pǎo*: 'The dog runs', or 我 们[們] 走 吧 *wǒmen zǒu ba*: 'Let's go' in the active group, and *hūa hóng*: 'The flower is red' or 她 很 漂 亮 *tā hěn piàoliang*: 'She is very pretty' in the adjectival group. Both can follow adverbs; thus 'to run quickly' is 快 跑 *kuài pǎo*, '[to be] very beautiful' is 非 常 漂 亮 *fēicháng piàoliang*. Both groups may also take suffixed particles (see

About Chinese

Aspect). One difference between their use is that adverbs of degree (like 很 *hěn*: 'very', 太 *tài*: 'too', 十 分 *shī-fen*: 'completely') appear before adjective-verbs but generally not before active verbs unless these cover mental or emotional processes (thus one might say *wǒ hěn xiǎng qù*: 'I very much want to go', with *hěn* as the adverb 'very'). Secondly, although both groups may repeat or reduplicate to give a modified meaning (看 看 *kàn-kan*: 'to have a look', 好 好 的 *hǎohāode*: 'thoroughly'), when a compound verb does so, the repetition is different. Active verbs repeat in entirety (*xiūxi xiūxi*: 'to have a little rest', from 休 息 *xiūxi*: 'to rest'), where adjectives repeat their separate parts (*gāngan jìngjing*, a stronger version of 干 [乾] 淨 *gānjìng*: 'clean').

One other difference between the two groups involves *hūa hóng* again. For all the usefulness of the example, Chinese is no more likely to make adjective-predicates out of the air, neutrally, than is any other language; 'The flower is red' would seldom be heard without further comment. Adjective-predicates are only met unmodifiedly when there is already, or shortly will be, an extra sense of comparison or comment. When there is not, they modify.

The most usual modifier is *hěn*, often wrongly translated as 'very'. It does mean 'very' when emphasis demands this, but it may equally be neutral. 这 [這] 个 [個] 很 好 *zhèige hěn hǎo* does not have to mean 'This is very good', but merely 'This is good'. And if there is some real comparison, or a question, or a negative, then this generalized, almost formal *hěn* may be dropped: 这 [這] 个 [個] 好 ， 那 个 [個] 不 好 *zhèige hǎo, nèige bùhǎo* ('This is good, that's not'), 这 [這] 个 [個] 好 吗 [嗎] ？ *zhèige hǎo ma?* ('Is this good?'), and 这 [這] 个 [個] 不 好 *zhèige bùhǎo* ('This isn't good'), none of which need *hěn* between subject and predicate. Other adverbs of degree behave more regularly.

Verbs of the active group can appear unadorned without any such extra sense of comparison or comment. They form independent ideas in themselves: *gǒu pǎo*: 'The dog is running'. Since they do not usually deal with measurable units, adverbs used with them are of quality rather than of degree, 你 快 跑 吧 *nǐ kuài pǎo ba*: 'You'd better run quickly' being more usual.

Measures

Numbers and measures do more work in Chinese than is asked of them in Western languages.

Script forms for numerals are among the simplest and oldest of Chinese characters (ignoring the elaborate variants used to discourage forgery on bank-notes and legal documents). Before joining with a noun, the common numerals interpose a measure-word. A great many of these exist, each used with a particular class of noun particularly associated with it. There is no exact equivalent of the measure-word in Western languages. It has three functions, the first two of which need special attention since they partly overlap with Western forms.

Measure-words may first be quantitative units used with a wide variety of nouns for 'how much' of something divisible: 'piece of', 'bowl of'. Secondly, measure-words are identifiers, stressing the nature as well as the units of a noun, somewhat as does 'hand' in the English 'a hand of cards'. Functionally these enumerative and descriptive uses coincide.

In English, the second use is generally a collective noun, found with or else implying the plural: 'a school of porpoises'. The Chinese measure-word in contrast has both singular and plural senses. It is not necessarily an enumerator; combined with an indicative element, it can become a pronoun or demonstrative noun-substitute (the element may also be a numeral).

Measure-words often have pictorial symbolism: 头 [頭] *tóu*: 'head' used for 'cow' is one example, but they may also express one quality of their particular noun-group with a less obvious connexion. So 张 [張] *zhāng*: 'to stretch' is the measure for a flat-surfaced noun (bed, table, picture, paper, animal hide) placed between numeral or indicator and the noun in question: 两 [兩] 张 [張] 纸 [紙] *liǎng zhāng zhǐ*: 'two sheets of paper', 这 [這] 张 [張] 画 [畫] *zhèi zhāng huàr*: 'this picture', 那 四 百 张 [張] 牛 皮 *nèi sìbǎizhāng níupí*: 'those 400 cow-hides'.

Measure-words may have originated from the need to

distinguish homophones for words in common use. If two nouns sound the same (as do 'shirt' and 'mountain', both *shān*) or almost the same ('chair', *yǐzi*, and 'soap', *yízi*), then an outside aid to clarify would anyway be necessary. 'Shirt' conveniently takes a different measure-word (件 *jiàn*) from that of 'mountain' (座 *zuò*); 'chair' likewise diverges from 'soap'.

The Chinese indefinite article may be said to be the measure-word. Thus the phrase 一 张 [張] 纸 [紙] *yì zhāng zhǐ*, as well as being an enumerative 'one sheet of paper', may also express the indefinite 'a sheet'. It may stand for a pre-stated noun: 我 只 要 那 本 书 [書] *wǒ zhǐ yào nèiběn (shū)*: 'I just want that one' (assuming the context of 'books').

Where the student's difficulty lies is not in the large number of such measures (there are perhaps as many in English) but in exploiting them to the full and with the noun-group of particular association. This last can seem hard. How is it that 条 [條] *tiáo* (another 'long' measure, mainly for roads and rivers) is associated with *gǒu*: 'dog'? Or 把 *bǎ* (the measure for 'graspable' things) with chairs, knives, brushes and keys, but not with pens, rifles, chopsticks, pencils or ropes? How does one remember 副 *fù* (a pair of glasses), 双 [雙] *shuāng* (a pair of shoes) and 对 [對] *dùi* (a pair of twins)? Fortunately there are a few catch-all measures applicable to a wide range of nouns. The most common of these are 个 [個] *gè* and 件 *jiàn*, which (with 种 [種] *zhǒng*) are used with hundreds of frequent nouns. Moreover, specialist fields (modern science, for example) make few additions to the stock of measure-words in general use.

What is more common in the sciences is the third function of measures (as distinct from measure-words), this being to state exact amounts of time, light, distance, weight, etc. (Peking has gone metric, and the old confusion of 'market-system' measures, traditional Chinese units, and Anglo-American loaned terms is no more.) One overlap to notice with these real measures is the small group which are also common nouns: 年 *nián*: 'year', 斤 *jīn*: 'catty',* are two. They normally, as nouns, do not themselves take a measure-word (*gè*); 'two catties' is usually *liǎng jīn*, 'five years' is *wǔ nián*. These distinctions are well expressed by the dual possibilities of 尺 *chǐ*: 'foot', which can mean either 'a footrule' or 'one foot (in length)' according to whether or not it has its measure-word. It should not be forgotten that 'bowl', as well as standing for 'a bowl of something' (一 碗 饭 [飯] *yì wǎn fàn*: 'one-bowl-rice') and symbolizing 'a square meal' or 'the gravy-train' by extension, may also actually mean the bowl itself, empty of everything.

Finally the numerals. They contribute more to thought and imagery than do their Western counterparts. The Chinese are a number-conscious people. Many games involve counting; social, family or business hierarchies are numbered off according to rank and branch; pro-

* A unit of weight.

bably half of the countless Chinese proverbs use numbers for otherwise complex syntax or description. High numbers generally base on 万 (萬) *wàn*:'ten thousand', rather than on multiples of one thousand or fractions of a million or billion (though words for all these exist). *Wàn* is often used figuratively for any .vague large amount.

Pre-statements

Western languages differ in the degree of their inflexion. Chinese, with no inflexions and 'grammatical' case, uses word-order – even the ordering of whole phrases – to make clear many of the situations which in other languages require inflexion.

The normal order is subject-verb-object. Attributive adjectives come before the noun they qualify (in the *Verbal attributes* section they were predicates after their nouns). Expressions of time are placed sometimes before the subject, sometimes after it or a secondary verb, but at least generally ahead of the main verb and object. Place-expressions follow their place-relative-to, but unless used as predicates ('That man is over there') they come before the noun qualified: 铺 子 前 头 (頭) 那 个 (個) 人 *pùzi qiántou nèige rén*: 'that man in front of the shop', where *pùzi* = 'shop' and *qiántou* = 'in front of'.

Items in a fixed order, however, give a false idea of the nature of Chinese syntax. Inversion (particularly of the object) is the rule – indeed, the content of a whole sentence and the speaker's attitude to that content may invert in expressing itself. This is so usual that it produces no special emphasis of weight or rhetoric such as might be the effect in a Western language. A whole topic will be pre-stated: 'He-speak-Chinese, speak-very-well' says that 'He is very good at speaking Chinese'. Judged as a technical means alone, this form can reduce awkward crowding later in a sentence, but this sounds too much like making a virtue of necessity. The truth is that pre-statement of one kind or another is fundamental to Chinese thought and expression: 'Go-not-go, not-important' for 'It doesn't matter whether we go or not'. Applied to nouns, pre-statement is a way of stressing contrasts: 'Rice-there-is, noodles-not', while a double subject may be pre-stated in order later to be broken down or isolated: 'Those-two-men, one-is-Chinese, one-is-Japanese'. The topic may thus be a whole idea, a phrase, or one noun alone.

When inversion of the object occurs, it may be signalled by the particle 把 *bǎ*, one of the few 'formal' syllables that appear on their own and unsuffixed. A simple object may manage without *bǎ*: 忙 了 半 天， 水 都 没 喝 过 [過] 一 口 *mángle bàntīan, shuǐ dōu méi hēguo yì kǒu*: 'I've been so busy all day that I've not even drunk a mouthful of water' takes the object *shuǐ* ('water') and puts it at the place of greatest stress. The main verb *hēguo* then follows. When *bǎ* is used, however, it is placed directly in front of the object:

把 书 〔書〕 拿 给〔給〕我 *bǎ shū nágěi wǒ*: '*bǎ*-book-take-give-me', or 'Hand me the book'. The subject may be included: 我 把 书 〔書〕看 完 了 *wǒ bǎ shū kànwánle*: 'I have finished the book'.

Clearly, *bǎ* can only be used with transitive verbs, since it must have a direct object to invert. The object is usually specific: '*the*' book, not '*a*'. A monosyllabic main verb cannot stand alone after *bǎ* plus object, but must have some other element. Thus *bǎ shū gěi* and *wǒ bǎ shū kàn* are impossible; they sound unbalanced. Impersonal verbs like 象 〔像〕 *xiàng*: 'to resemble', 是 *shì*: 'to be' and 有 *yǒu*: 'to have' cannot use *bǎ*, nor can compound verbs of motion (回 家 *húijiā*: 'to return home' cannot be split to make *wǒ bǎ jiā húi*). Certain compound verbs of perception, emotion and thought also reject *bǎ*. 认 〔認〕识〔識〕 *rènshi* is 'to recognize, know', but *wǒ bǎ tā rènshi* is impossible, as is (with 知 道 *zhīdao*: 'to know') *bǎ qíngxing zhīdao*: 'to be familiar with the circumstances'. In these cases the explanation may be that such subjective verbs are too direct to be separated from their subjects by the *bǎ* construction.

This pre-statement and inversion may suggest that the Chinese 'think in a different direction'. Evidence favours 'large-to-small' as a direction of utterance, round general statements coming before particular comment. With dates, the year comes first, then month, then day. Similarly in fractions, the larger item precedes the smaller: 百 份 之 一 *bǎi fèn zhī yì*: 'hundred-

[93]

parts-of-one' or 'one per cent'. But do these formal differences prove anything? Perhaps the earlier example of 'Those-two-men . . .' is more significant. It seems typical of the Chinese mind to note of the men that they are two, a totality, before contrasting them as individuals, one Chinese, one Japanese. Compare this with the English pattern, 'One of those two men is Chinese . . .'. Chinese appears to stress allness rather than separateness. For example, 'Both he and she are tall' would use 都 *dōu*: 'all', and not the Western inclusive pattern 'both . . . and' (which does exist in Chinese but rather emphasizes separateness).

Against this evidence, possibly of a formal kind only, there is a rich source of exception: Chinese proverbs, in particular the pithy sayings often of four characters. Many of these indeed start with the larger item: 九 牛 一 毛 *jiǔ niú yì máo*: 'Nine-cows-one-hair' (='A drop in the ocean'); 百 闻 [聞] 不 如 一 见 [見] *bǎi wén bùrú yí jiàn*: 'To hear tell a hundred times is not as good as once seeing'; 三 心 二 意 *sān xīn èr yì*: 'In three hearts and two minds' (='to be confused'). But an equally convincing list of sayings with the smaller item first can be drawn up: 接 二 连 [連] 三 *jiē èr lián sān*: 'Join two to three' (='Step by step'); 贪 [貪] 小 失 大 *tān xiǎo shī dà*: 'To go for the small and lose the big'. It seems that any ordering of thoughts is due as much to a directional syntax and a fondness for antithesis as to the psychology or outlook of the Chinese.

Verb compounds

Verbs were earlier described as verbal attributes and active verbs. Compound verbs have also been mentioned. These are very common, and many seem in the way they are built up and used to cut across familiar Western categories of transitive/intransitive, separable/inseparable. The problem is only felt with compounds in the active group; but as this group anyway covers what the Westerner understands by 'verbs', it can serve as an approach to the whole topic.

Active verbs may be monosyllables, expressing simple actions and also many other verbal functions beyond these: 吃 *chī*: 'to eat', 作 *zuò*: 'to do, make', 比 *bǐ*: 'to compare' (like the English 'more than'), sometimes termed a co-verb, 会 [會] *huì*: 'to know how to' (an auxiliary), and 给 [給] *gěi*: 'to give' (already met on page 93 in *bǎ shū nágěi wǒ*: 'Hand me the book', where it was a co-verb used with *ná*: 'to take'; *gěi* can also be the preposition 'for').

A large number of these monosyllable verbs are found linked closely to another element. It is important to grasp what function this other element has in context, since on it will depend the total sense of the compounds. A direct object may form the second element: 看 书 [書] *kàn shū*: 'to read a book', 煮 饭 [飯] *zhǔ fàn*: 'to boil rice', 洗 脸 [臉] *xǐ liǎn*: 'to wash the face', 说 [說] 话 [話] *shūo huà*: 'to talk', 下 山 *xià shān*: 'to go down the hill', with verb and object in the same breath, as verbs. The object stays a genuine one, being often used with *bǎ* to invert. But it also may be dropped; for example, on the summit of a hill 下 山 了！ *xià shān le!*: 'Let's go down' could equally well be 下 去 了！ *xiàqü le!* (*qù* being the general verb for 'to go').

Equally common are verb compounds with the second element not (or not any longer) a genuine object: 休 息 *xiūxi*: 'to rest', 服 务 [務] *fúwù*: 'to serve', 攻 击 [擊] *gōngjī*: 'to attack'. Both elements may be verbs, adding up to a strengthened sense of either one of them (i.e. they are of the bound reduplicative type discussed on page 86). They cannot invert because there is no object, nor can they take another element in between themselves, or otherwise separate. Within this second group a variety seems perhaps to belong to the verb-plus-object first type, two examples being 回 家 *húijīa*: 'to go home' and 睡 觉 [覺] *shùijiào*: 'to sleep'. While never inverting their second element, these need not always keep strictly together; thus, 'to sleep for a little' separates for the time-measure to come between its two parts.

With the more usual verb-object compound there are often two senses to be felt: the general and the restricted. Western transitives like 'to move house' or 'to drive a car' can easily seem intransitives (generalized by dropping their objects). So can a number of Chinese verbs for everyday actions, but the difference is that, in so seeming, they *keep* their object even closer than before.

With the example of 饭〔飯〕 *fàn*: literally 'cooked rice', the effect is as follows: *zhǔ fàn* means 'to boil rice', in the restricted sense of preparing rice, no more; *fàn*, however, is also the general term for food of any kind that may form a meal, whether it be rice, soup, meat, fish or all of these together. So that to ask someone 'to come and eat rice' (请〔請〕人 来〔來〕吃 饭〔飯〕 *qǐng rén lái chī fàn*) is the usual way to phrase an invitation for a meal – to ask someone *to come and eat*, in short. *chīfàn* thus forms a verbal compound with a more general sense than its words give when taken literally. The object is made less particularized.

In other cases an historical explanation accounts for compounds with this general meaning: 念 书〔書〕 *niànshū*: 'to study' literally means 'to read book aloud', which was how the pupil learned the classics. This verb is still used today in a completely generalized sense regardless of whether the 'reading' is done aloud (it very often is, in a Chinese school).

Such verbs are picturesque and typical. Three technical points are to be noted. When the object is particularized in any but the very simplest way, the general sense is lost and the expression once more looks fully transitive. Thus, 作 饭〔飯〕 *zuòfàn* is 'to cook (anything)', but 她 把 三 个〔個〕人 的 饭〔飯〕 作 好 了 *tā bǎ sānge rénde fàn zuòhǎole* says specifically that 'she has *prepared rice* for three people', both the verb and the object being modified away from the general meaning of *zuòfàn*. This in English might involve a change of verb; for example, 说 [說] 话 [話] *shuō-huà* is 'to talk', but 说 [說] 那 句 话 [話] 真 不 容 易 [易] *shuō nèiju huà zhēn bùróngyi*, a particularized object, means 'To *say* that sentence is very difficult'.

Secondly, a few of these verb compounds, in particular those formed with 有 *yǒu*: 'to have', can very easily go over to being adjectives. If 有 钱 [錢] *yǒu qián* means 'have-money' or 'to be rich', then it is only a step to use *yǒuqián* adjectivally, as in 他 很 有 钱 [錢] *tā hěn yǒuqián*: 'he is rich'.

Lastly, a translation point. Sometimes a babu style will be attempted to give 'Chinese' colour to the English version. This is mistaken. What is essentially Chinese, namely the verb and its fused unparticularized object, demands translation by the simplest English verb, preferably with no object. The Chinese expression 写 [寫] 字 *xiě zì* is not 'to write characters', but 'to write'; only an added 'Chinese' or 'Japanese' can justify a translation by 'characters'. Also, 看戏 [戲] *kàn xì* need not mean 'to watch a play'; it might be said of various public entertainments: 我 们 [們] 出 去 看 戏 [戲] 吧 *wǒmen chūqù kàn xì ba*: 'Let's go out to a show' (i.e. cinema, opera, play, ballet, boxing-match, etc.). In translation, therefore, this may concern accuracy as much as style.

Overloading

'Chinese has no grammar' usually implies that it lacks tenses, declensions, formalized parts of speech, and so on. This is true, but since any language must have recurring patterns (the wider meaning of grammar), to be of any real help the statement needs interpreting otherwise. What it can more usefully say is that those Chinese patterns which do exist are made to carry too heavy a load in too many different areas.

This is specially true of one 'formal' particle, 的 *de*. Linked to a noun, it shows possession: 他 的 书 [書] *tāde shū*: 'his book', like English '—'s' or '—s''. Then, just as the English possessive may be viewed adjectivally ('What *kind* of book? His book'), so *de* may extend into a genuine adjective; it may do so even when a straight possessive seems required (compare 中 国 [國] 地 理 *zhōngguó dìlǐ*: 'China-geography' with 中 国 [國] 的 地 理 *zhōngguóde dìlǐ*: 'Chinese geography', which have virtually identical meanings). As attributes, adjectives formed with *de* are placed before their nouns: 红 [紅] 的 花 *hóngde hūa*: 'red flowers'. A further extension of *de* can match the English agent-suffixes -or and -er (as in 'doctor'). This usually involves a verb-object compound: 作 饭 [飯] 的 *zuòfànde*: 'a cook', 念 书 [書] 的 *niànshūde*: 'students'. Yet another use of *de* is as time-measure: 他 每 天 看 三 个 [個] 钟 [鐘] 头 [頭] 的 书 [書] *tā měitiān kàn sānge zhōngtoude shū*: 'He-each-day-reads-three-hours'-of-book'.

[99]

This might be thought to exhaust the formal possibilities of one monosyllable. It does not, but before looking at further uses for *de*, another much-used syllable must be studied. 是 *shì*: 'to be' was mentioned in *Verbal attributes* as the copula or equative verb. Where *shì* is found between two nouns, it simply links them: 他 是 我 朋 友 *tā shi wǒ péngyǒu*: 'He is my friend'. If the link is of a noun to an adjective, then that quality (or the possession of it) is emphasized in some way: 那 个 〔個〕孩 子 是 聪 〔聰〕明 *nèige háizi shi cōngmíng*: 'That child's clever'. *shì* is also the English 'yes' in answering positively phrased questions: 你 是 英 国 〔國〕人 吗 〔嗎〕? 是 *nǐ shi yīngguó rén ma? shì*: 'Are you English? Yes'. There are some half-dozen other uses for *shì* which concern spoken emphasis rather than any formal difference in the meaning of the verb. Thus, 她 是 来 〔來〕看 你 ， 不 是 来 〔來〕看 我 *tā shi lái kàn nǐ, bùshi lái kàn wǒ*: 'She's come to see you, not me'; 这 〔這〕东 〔東〕西 好 是 好 ， 可 是 太 贵 〔貴〕*zhèi dōngxi hǎo shi hǎo, kèshi tài gùi*: 'That thing's good all right, but too expensive'; 是 人 都 知 道 他 靠 不 住 *shi rén dōu zhīdao tā kàobuzhù*: 'Everyone knows he's unreliable'. So *shi* may cover shades of contrast or emphasis expressed by the English 'indeed', 'each and every', 'no matter what', etc. These are overtones, as against its strictly equative use in 二 加 二 是 四 *èr jīa èr shi sì*: 'Two and two make four'.

Combinations of *shi* and *de* within a phrase are frequent. 他 是 作 买 [買] 卖 [賣] 的 *tā shi zuò mǎimàide*: 'He is a businessman' simply identifies the subject. Then the combination may move an adjective from the attributive to the predicative position (that is, from before the noun to after it), giving the noun more weight: 那 些 书 [書] 是 新 的 *nèixie shū shi xīnde*: 'Those books are (the) new (ones)'. But there is a special use of the *shi . . . de* pattern which alters the two syllables almost by a chemical change. This, its circumstantial use, tells how, when, where, by what means the main action occurred, and removes all emphasis from the subject.

In Chinese, 'conveyance' travel generally involves the verb 坐 *zuò*: 'to sit', and a main verb such as 来 [來] *lái*: 'to come'. Thus, 'Did he come by bus?' is pidgin-translated as 'He-*shi*-sit-bus-come-*de?*'. All conveyance-ideas, like 坐 飞 [飛] 机 [機] *zuò fēijī*: 'by plane', 坐 火 车 [車] *zuò huǒchē*: 'by train', may take *shi . . . de* as their framework when describing past, present or future journeys: 他 们 [們] 是 坐 汽 车 [車] 去 的 *tāmen shi zuò qìchē qùde*: 'They went by car'. 'Time-when' ideas follow this. 他 是 今 天 到 的 *tā shi jīntīan dàode*: 'He got here today'. The aim of his coming may also do so: 他 是 到 这 [這] 儿 [兒] 来 [來] 念 书 [書] 的 *tā shi dào zhèr lái niànshū de*: 'He has come here to study' shares the pattern.

'Place-where' may likewise be emphasized. 他 是 在 北 京 念 的 书 [書] *tā shi zài Běijǐng niàn de shū* says that he studied, but more importantly that he studied in Peking (*zài Běijīng*) rather than else-where.

These patterns are to some extent variable. *shi* may often be dropped, particularly in speech, but only when the sentence is formed positively. So *tā zuò fēijī láide*: 'He came by plane' is possible, but for 'He didn't come by plane' the phrase *tā búshi . . . de* and not *tā búzuò . . . de* would be necessary. Then there is flexibility in the plac-ing of *de*, when the verb is a separable verb-object com-pound: one hears *tā shi zài Běijīng niànshūde* as well as the *. . . niàn de shū* given above, though the first may have a slightly different emphasis, something of 'he studied, didn't have a job'. It seems that where this first emphasis is wanted, the verb-object must not be separated by *de*; where the point is at once fully made following *shi*, then *de*'s position does not matter.

In these uses for circumstance, the emphasis is trans-ferred to the action, and the result is an adverbial phrase. But what of *de* in its earlier use of signalling adjectives, that is, describing nouns rather than actions? The 'Peking' example, said to concern the circumstances of an action, may equally well be viewed as a description of the subject. *tā shi zài Běijīng niànshūde* may say 'He is the one who studied in Peking' – that man and no other. The whole predicate, in this sense, is a long sub-stantive phrase relating to the subject *tā* at one end and to an implied *rén*: 'man' at the other: 'he is the studied-in-Peking man'. Only spoken emphasis can make clear such a sense – though this time the equative *shi* cannot be dropped, and this helps to anchor the new meaning.

Thus even the limited, circumstantial pattern of *shi ... de* has its overtones and ambiguities. The many uses, separately and together, of *shi* and *de* contribute to this devaluation of linguistic currency, especially so in *bái huà* which needs them more than does the literary language. A Chinese reading *bái huà* aloud can discover, halfway through a long *shi ... de* phrase, that he has stressed the wrong part of it. The effect is that of reading wrong punctuation into a Western sentence: the damage is discovered too late to be put right. Before condemning Chinese for this weakness, however, one should remember that the English 'Did he come by plane today?' may have many possible senses, only anchored by spoken emphasis; but for all that, the Western languages are richer in formally distinct alternatives.

Antithesis

If pre-statement characterizes thought and syntax, then antithesis marks both syntax – the ordering of words – and formal elements in these words themselves. It is a quality seen most clearly in the standard pattern for phrasing questions.

Chinese, apparently more ambiguous than Western languages, appears again to emphasize this by its use of antithesis. Its flavour is marked by the placing together of contrasts within a single word, phrase, sentence or paragraph. The traditional 'eight-legged essay', introduced during the Ming dynasty, taught students to present an idea and at once to balance it with an opposite. Chinese philosophy and natural science rely on much the same contrast of forces.

The question-pattern shows this in action at the simplest level. The neutral question-particle 吗 〔嗎〕 *ma* has already been met. Any question requiring a 'yes-no' answer (that is, any not using an interrogative such as 'who?' or 'where?') may be formed simply by placing *ma* at the end of a statement: 他 老 *tā lǎo*: 'He is old'; 他 老 吗 〔嗎〕? *tā lǎo ma?*: 'Is he old?'. More polite, more 'Chinese', is the choice-pattern, which drops *ma* and rephrases the statement into positive and negative; thus, 他 老 不 老? *tā lǎo bùlǎo?* The answer then takes one or other of these choices in reply: 〔他〕不 老 *(tā) bùlǎo*: 'No, (he's) not old', or 〔他〕老 *(tā) lǎo*: 'Yes, (he) is old'. The exact form of reply varies with the framing of the choice, but the latter's neutrality remains and the choice is a free one. 你 敢 不 敢 去 对 〔對〕他 说 〔説〕? *nǐ gǎn bùgǎn qù dùi tā shūo?*: 'Do you dare to go and say (it) to him?', for example, has three verbs, but the only relevant choice is between *gǎn*: 'to dare' and its negative *bùgǎn*, neither *qù*: 'to go' or *shūo*: 'to speak' being involved. 他 是 美 国 〔國〕人 不 是? *tā shi měigúo rén búshi?*: 'He's an American, isn't he?'

shows the two choices widely separated, *tā shibushi měiguó rén?* being equally correct. The choice-type pattern is also used for antitheses which are less questions than open alternatives: 你 说[説]— 我 们 [們] 今 天 去 不 去 *nǐ shūo – wǒmen jīntīan qù buqù*: 'You say (if) we're to go today or not'. This pattern, questioning or testing, can only be used when real positive and negative verbs are postulated. Where the verb is fixed and unquestionable, as in 'Does he live in Peking or Shanghai?', the pattern is not found.

Opposites placed together run right through the language. In building abstract nouns for the amount or degree of a quality, spoken Chinese (less often the written language) will use two extremes together in one word, such as 高 矮 *gāoǎi*: 'height', made up of 高 *gāo*: 'tall' and 矮 *ǎi*: 'low', 长 [長] 短 *chángduǎn*: 'length' ('long-short'), 宽 [寬] 窄 *kūanzhǎi*: 'breadth' ('broad-narrow'), and 大 小 *dàxiǎo*: 'size' ('big-small'). Such abstracts are usually kept for measurable, pictorial qualities. They fit these well, because discussion of length, height, etc., does best to avoid loaded terms which in themselves suggest that the item concerned *is* long or high. The pattern, here and in questions, leaves the issue open.

Predictably, there are several words for 'approximately' made up in this way: 上 下 *shàngxià*: 'up-down', and 左 右 *zǔoyòu*: 'left-right' are two. A number of concrete nouns and active verbs consist if not of direct opposites, then of contrasts: 操 纵 [縱] *cāozòng*:

'grasp-relax' for 'to control', and 影 响 [響] *yǐng-xiǎng*: 'shadow-echo' for 'influence'.

Question-patterns are only one syntactic use for antithesis. Several thousand sayings (the *chéngyǔ* of page 78) express almost as much by balancing opposites as by the four characters they comprise. Modern Chinese, without many Western clause-building means, continues this use of antithetical statement, despite Peking's trend to longer, more loosely knitted sentences.

The impression may now have been given that the language's best resources lie in contrasted opposites, all such opposites adding up to non-committed neutrality. This is not the whole story. Extremes of quality, for example, may sometimes be combined to give a very emphatic sense indeed. 我 高 低 不 走 *wǒ gāo dī* ('high-low') *bùzǒu* says 'Nothing on earth will make me go', with 'high-low' as the emphatic. Other instances are 他 始 终 [終] 不 明 白 *tā shǐ zhōng* ('beginning-end') *bùmíngbai*: 'He'll simply never understand', and 你 早 晚 得 来 [來] 见 [見] 我 *nǐ zǎo wǎn* ('early-late') *děi lái jiàn wǒ*: 'Sooner or later you'll have to come and see me'. Then there is the uniquely Chinese pivot-word 反 正 *fǎnzhèng*: 'contrary-upright', translatable by 'in any case' but also (with negative emphasis) by the sense of 'come what may (I won't)'. Emphasis is thus by no means always neutral. Indeed, the language's suitability for abstracts in the moral or philosophical area is arguable. It is hard, for example, to discuss ideas of 'goodness', 'value', or 'beauty' without relating these to objects either possessing or lacking them. Translators have to coin new ways of expressing these ideas, unless they adopt for them the traditional Confucian expressions which are far from suitable. One neutral abstract, 好 坏 [壞] *hǎohuài*: 'good-bad', does exist for 'goodness', but its use is still not as a philosopher would wish it.

Directionals

Concern for 'position relative to' is much in evidence. The basic verbs of motion are few and are worked hard. They must act in relation to a central point of interest and be filled out with added elements if they are to express overtones of 'to' and 'from'. Even where a specific motion-verb exists, such as 'to remove (one's home and possessions)', it will be reinforced with a directional element.

These are 来 [來] *lái*: 'to come' and 去 *qù*: 'to go'. Freely used as appendages to other verbs, they may appear at times to produce overstatements, but as a rule bear little weight. They further have many extended or figurative senses (see *Resultatives*). Whatever the context, they always show (formally at least) this concern for 'towards where' or 'away from where'. The speaker, or his topic, is always at the centre of things, and syntax operates directionally.

This has been noted in such 'typically Chinese' ideas as the name of China itself: 中 国 [國] *zhōngguó*, 'middle country', claimed to tell one more about the Chinese than does 'Mediterranean' about the Romans. *zhōngguó* may or may not have implied that China was the centre of the world; its geographical position was in the midst of barbarians to north and south and desert and sea to west and east, so the name would fit on that level alone. However, archaic expressions for 'the civilized world' (天 下 *tiānxià*: 'all under heaven') and for lands outside it (海 外 *hǎiwài*: 'beyond the seas') do suggest a well-centralized view of the universe. In modern Chinese, 这 [這] 儿 [兒] *zhèr* and 那 儿 [兒] *nèr* ('here' and 'there'), and *lái* and *qù* ('come' and 'go') all mean in themselves 'to the speaker' or 'away from the speaker'. They pair off to make directional statements, often adding another element (pronoun, preposition, co-verb) to be yet more clear. Thus, 请 [請] 他 到 我 这 [這] 儿 [兒] 来 [來] *qǐng tā dào wǒ zhèr lái*: 'Ask him to come here' has three directionals – or four if the pronoun *wǒ*: '(to) me' is counted – in a total of six words.

In practice the important question is 'relative to whom?'. For instance, the apparently independent verb 回 *húi*: 'to return' must specify its return as 'coming to' or 'going to'. 他 回 到 那 儿 [兒] 去 *tā húidào nèr qù*: 'He-return-to-there-goes' clearly says 'away from here', but in 他 回 到 这 [這] 儿 [兒] 来 [來] *tā húidào zhèr lái* the return is *to* the speaker or point of identification.

An action like removing one's hat must be given coordinates on this syntactic map. 请 [請] 你 把 帽 子 拿 下 来 [來] *qǐng nǐ bǎ màozi náxiàlái*: 'Please-your-hat-take-down-come' is the way to address a lady blocking one's view; note the use of *lái*, implying 'to me'. She in turn says *wǒ bǎ màozi náxiàláile*: 'I have taken off my hat', the action of taking off being relative to her, hence *lái* again. But a third person, outside the incident, says *tā bǎ màozi náxiàqùle*, since he was not involved and to his view the hat 'went' down (*xiàqùle*), away from him. Point of interest is thus paramount.

Initially, the point may not always seem identifiable. When telephoning a friend and learning that he is out, how should 'When will he return?' be asked? Should it be 回 来 [來] *húilai*, as seen by the person answering the telephone? Or should the action be viewed as going away from where the friend is now, that is, 回 去 *húiqù*? The odds are on *húilai* (*húiqù* would tend to mean 'set out to return'). Fortunately, once the principle of *lái* and *qù* has been grasped, few situations will give rise to such doubts, since it is only English lack of practice in such thinking that causes the difficulty.

Other directional elements form clusters with the verbs of motion. Like the verb-object compounds (page 97), these clusters may be of varying degrees of firmness, the elements changing in function with their closeness to the verb. Two elements are 从 [從] *cóng* and 到 *dào*, often translated by prepositions, 'from' and 'to'. Thus, 从 [從] 前 边 [邊] 儿 [兒] 来 [來] *cóng qiánbīar lái*: 'come from in front', and 到 后[後]边[邊] 儿[兒] 去 *dào hòubīar qù* 'go to the back', show the 'place-where-at' expressions (formed on *-bīar*, *-tóu* or *-miàn*) in use as 'place-from-or-to-where' ideas with *cóng*, *dào* and the verb. Apart from a few figurative uses, *cóng* keeps to that form. *dào*, however, is also an intransitive verb in its own right. It is used alone, as in 他 今 天 到 了 *tā jīntian dàole*: 'He arrived to-day'. More often it becomes a firm part of a complete verbal expression, that is, a co-verb. 'To move (some-thing)' is 搬 *bān*, 'to move something somewhere' is *bāndao*, which when given its appropriate *qù* or *lái* can become 'to remove to' a specified place: 'We are mov-ing to Peking' is 我 们[們] 搬 到 北 京 去 *wǒmen bāndao Běijīng qù*. Elsewhere movement given formal expression may be mental rather than physical: 'Today we'll read to page 14': 我 们[們] 今 天 念 到 第 十 四 页[頁] *wǒmen jīntian niàndao di shìsì yè*. *dào* thus coalesces with many active verbs covering the attainment of a given point, whether in time, place, degree or result.

A problem with the co-verbs may be to hook the cor-rect part of the sentence onto them. The hook in Eng-lish may not be appropriate; for 'I am not going to Peking', instinctive translation puts the negative with 'going', but the Chinese 我 不 到 北 京 去 *wǒ búdào Běijīng qù* negates *dào*, the co-verb, not *qù*. Similarly the verbs of motion (*húi*, *bān*) are linked to *dào* and not to the directional verbs *lái/qù*. One should

say 他 今 天 回 到 这 [這] 儿 [兒] 来 [來]
tā jīntian húidao zhèr lái: 'He's coming back (here) to-day' (and not ... *dào zhèr húilai*); *wǒmen bāndao Běijīng qù*: 'We are moving to Peking' (and not ... *dao Běijīng bānqù*). When *dào* is used in a verbal idea, it thus has the attraction-power which otherwise *lái* and *qù* possess.

With this apparent Chinese overstatement on direction, it would be helpful if these various means were to distinguish the different *stages* of an identical action. They do not do so. 'When are you arriving in Peking?' may use *dào* as a single verb: 你 什 [甚] 么 [麼] 时 [時] 候 到 北 京 的 *nǐ shénma shíhou dào Běijīng de?*, to show that what is asked is the moment of arrival, but elsewhere the added verbal elements do not coalesce on a time basis. Fine nuances such as 'When did you go (i.e. set out from here) to Peking?', 'Are you going (i.e. on your way now) to Peking?', and 'When will you be going (i.e. in future) to Peking?' are all constructed on the same pattern, which cannot alter internally to give a system of progression or of tense-changes.

Aspect

The means of showing 'time-when' are indeed few. Moreover, little formal attention is paid to time-sequence, the language preferring to order events syntactically with their chronological succession built in.

This means that a few time-adverbs ('now', 'yesterday', 'later', etc.) carry much of the weight of Western tenses. For example, 'I do not know if he went yesterday, is going today, or will go tomorrow' translates as 我 不 知道,他 昨 天 去·今 天 去, 还 [還] 是 明 天 去 *wǒ bùzhīdào tā zuótian qù, jīntian qù, háishi míngtian qù*, and changes its verb no more than does the question 'Do you drink tea with milk, rum or lemon?'. The verb stays unaltered. Provided the state of an action's completeness is expressed and the time-context clear, tense is irrelevant.

What replaces it is concern for state of completeness. Interest centres on finality or continuance. This pointing to the 'aspect' of an action may be clearer than a Western tense, as witness 'China has had a communist government since 1949' (and still has), identical in form with 'China has had many dynasties'. The difference in meaning is expressed in Chinese by one aspect-particle.

First and most general of these particles is the suffix 了 *-le*. This may follow either verb or sentence, or both, giving a 'perfective' aspect of the kind found in the English 'did', 'has done', 'had done', 'has been done', 'will have done', 'having done', formed on a main active verb to stress finality, either real or potential. Thus, used singly after a simple active verb: 票 都 买 [買] 了 吗 [嗎]? 买 [買] 了· *piào dōu mǎile ma? mǎile*: 'Have (you) bought the tickets? Yes (have bought)', or: 他 己 经 [經] 去 了 没 有? *tā yǐjing qùle méiyou?*: 'Has he gone already or not?'. Used after an adjective-verb, *-le* may signal a change of amount or degree: 他 高 了 一 寸 *tā gāole yi cùn*: 'He has grown an inch', or 今 天 暖 和 了 一 点 [點] 儿 [兒] *jīntian nuǎnhele yìdi-ăr*: 'It's got a little warmer today'. Then *-le* may reflect a change in the condition or state of the subject. After a simple active verb, negated, the effect is 'not any more', as in 我 不 要 了 *wǒ búyàole*: 'I don't want any more'; used with verb-object constructions the sense may be positive: 他 改 了 主 意 *tā gǎile zhúyì*: 'He has changed his mind'.

Apart from the above, a single *-le* is seldom used to show a completed past-tense action, or when it is, then reference to stated circumstances is usual, as in: 后 [後] 来 [來] 闭 [閉] 会 [會] 了 *hòulái bì hùi le*: 'Later [after that] they closed the meeting', or 吃 了 谢 谢 [謝 謝] *chīle, xièxie*: 'I've eaten, thanks' (in answer to 'Have you eaten a meal?'). Without such circumstances a double *le* is more usual, once within the sentence immediately after the verb, once at sentence-end. This is common with verb-object constructions. For example, a frequent midday greeting is 你 吃 了 饭 [飯] 了 吗 [嗎]? *nǐ chīle fàn le ma?* (literally 'Have you eaten?'). The past tense in such an idiom need not be very strong. Where there is a wish to stress completeness or finality, however, this double *le* may come near to a Western perfect or pluperfect, as in: 可 是 已 经 [經] 闭 [閉] 了 会 [會] 了 *kěshi yǐjing bìle hùi le*: 'But the meeting's already been closed'

About Chinese

(so the measure cannot go through), or 不 过 [過] 他 昨 天 买 [買] 了 票 了 *búguò tā zuótian mǎile piào le*: 'But he bought the tickets yesterday' (so we should not change our plans now). Then, two *le* particles in one sentence may show an ordering of events, particularly when 就 *jiù*: 'then' is used: 闭 [閉] 了 会 [會], 他 们 [們] 就 走 了 *bì le huì, tāmen jiù zǒule*: 'After the meeting had been closed, they left'.

Examples of aspect have so far been 'past tense'. *-le* also has a 'future' aspect, supplementing the function of future auxiliaries such as 要 *yào*: 'to intend to' and 想 *xiǎng*: 'to plan to, feel like'. The single *-le* may indicate an imminent event, or one to be desired: 快 下 雨 了 *kuài xià yǔ le*: 'Soon-down-rain-*le*' for 'It looks like rain', and 算 了 吧! *suànle ba!* for 'Forget it!' (*-le* being imperative). Using *jiù*: 'then', the ordering of two events may also be of a future kind: 你 们 [們] 谈 [談] 完 了, 我 们 [們] 就 走 *nǐmen tánwánle, wǒmen jiù zǒu*: 'When you've finished chatting, we'll go'.

The double *le* may signal an action that began in the past and is expected to continue into the future. 会 [會] 议 [議] 开 [開] 了 三 次 了 *huìyì kāile sān cì le*: 'The meeting has sat three times' (and will re-convene tomorrow); 我 念 中 文, 念 了 三 个 [個] 月 了 *wǒ niàn zhōngwén, niànle sānge yuè le*: 'I have been studying written Chinese for three months' (and intend to go on).

This last use differs from that of another suffix:

过 [過] -*gùo*: 'to have done something *in the past*'. The difference between *le* and *gùo* is clear in their primary meanings as 'free' words. *le* (or the 'free' word *liǎo*) means 'to finish', and (as -*liǎo*, the complement to active verbs) it indicates a full or successful conclusion. The primary meaning of *gùo*, however, is 'to pass, cross, ford'; 请 [請] 你 过 [過] 来 [來] *qǐng nǐ gùolái*: 'Please come over here' shows its meaning as an active verb. When something has been crossed, or experienced, one looks back across the gulf that separates 'now' from 'then', and this is the force of -*gùo* when used as a suffix. 你 去 过 [過] 中 国 [國] 没 有? *nǐ qùguo zhōnggúo méiyou?* asks 'Have you ever been to China?' (in your life), whereas 你 去 中 国 [國] 了 没 有? *nǐ qù zhōnggúo le méiyou?*: '...did you go to China?' asks if you went there at some particular time, say in March last year.

General experience widely viewed is the normal context for -*gùo*, but there may also be some time-limit within which -*gùo* has a more restricted sense. Looking back on a whole day, 今 天 我 没 见 [見] 过 [過] 他 *jīntian wǒ méijiànguo tā*: 'I didn't see him (once) today' is possible, 'day' standing for a complete period (similarly 'month', 'term', 'year', etc.). -*gùo* can also attach itself to a verb and be absorbed by it until its specifically past sense disappears; it will then be used with -*le* as other verbs: 今 天 我 见 [見] 过 [過] 他 了 *jīntian wǒ jiànguo tā le:* 'I saw him today'. As a suffix -*gùo* points to altered circumstances, where

-le suggests they are the same as at the action. Compare
我 去 年 到 过 [過] 上 海 *wǒ qùnián dàoguo Shànghǎi*: 'I went to Shanghai last year' (and am no longer there) with 我 去 年 就 到 了 上 海 *wǒ qùnián jiù dàole Shànghǎi* (and am still there now).

As *-le* and *-gùo* show finality, so the particles *zhe* and *ne* show continuance, or one action taking place alongside another.

The suffix *-zhe* matches the English participle '-ing', as in 'talking', 'reading', etc. (Pronounced as 着 *-zháo*, and used with an active verb, it may show an end-result, that of succeeding to do something; compare the *le/liǎo* switch, and see also *Resultatives*.) But as *-zhe*, it shows an action in progress with another: 他 看 着 书 [書] 吃 饭 [飯] *tā kànzhe shū chīfàn*: 'He eats while reading', or continuance of one action alone: 他 一 定 还 [還] 等 着 我 们 [們] 呢 *tā yídìng hái děngzhe wǒmen ne*: 'He's sure to be still waiting for us'.

This example introduces the floating particle 呢 *ne*, which, in leaving an action open, may be said to have the opposite effect to that of *-le*, which closes one. 他 们 [們] 正 在 谈 [談] 话 [話] 呢 *tāmen zhèngzai tán huà ne* means 'They are in the middle of talking'. When used in a negative context, *ne* serves to hold up an action, somewhat like the English 'still not': 我 还 [還] 没 到 中 国 [國] 去 过 [過] 呢 *wǒ hái méidao zhōngguó qùguo ne*: 'I've not yet been to China', or 他 还 [還] 没 买 [買] 票 呢 *tā hái* *méimǎi piào ne*: 'He's still not bought the tickets'. So *ne* is no more limited to one 'tense' than is *-le*.

Aspect is one of the few recognizably 'Chinese' grammatical concepts. It need not relate to 'time-when', though in practice it often does. Nor need it cover ideas of 'time relative to' ('Before going home, he . . .'), since these may be built on the lines of 'place relative to' phrases, with aspect unexpressed. Nor again is there any necessary comparison with Western conditionals or subjunctives, since these speculate on an action's possibility or result rather than on its completeness. For all this, the aspect uses discussed above are very distinct and, once mastered, hold fewer problems than do other apparently more 'Western' features of the language.

Relatives

One large weakness of the language is that it is not well disposed to form relative clauses. Even though (or perhaps because) Chinese words are often by their very nature already 'relative' to something, the formal weakness remains.

Inability to encapsulate is felt most of all in the modern language, especially when it translates foreign works or ideas. Classical Chinese asked nothing of syntax that it was incapable of giving and 'good style' lay in writing within these limits. But notably, such relative means as exist today are 'literary' in flavour, and modern *bái huà*, with different problems on hand, is in danger of becoming overblown and verbose from managing without formal relatives.

It is good Chinese to offer 他 买 [買] 的 那 些 东 [東] 西 *tā mǎide nèixe dōngxi*: 'he-buy-*de*-those-things' for 'those things which he bought . . .'. The relative pronoun is not translated, but neither is it missed. Similarly 'The chairman arrived precisely at three o'clock, when the meeting had been timed to start' becomes a *shi . . . de* phrase, with the relative 'when'-clause cleared after *shi* and before the main verb 'arrived'. Chinese thus avoids many situations expecting a relative in English. For 'You have to queue for food, which even then is inadequate' Chinese will make two statements: 'You queue for food. You have queued and the food is not enough'. It avoids long encapsulations like 'This rate is not for single but for married men, and as such you would be entitled to it but not your brother'. In Chinese, 'you are married' would probably be dealt with separately; your brother's position certainly would be.

The existing relative-forming means are among the oldest devices in the language, changed though their present force is. One such, 所 *sǔo*: (literally) 'place', is also the measure-word for buildings: 一 所 房 子 *yìsǔo fángzi*: 'a house'. Its most common use as a relative is to mean 'all' in adjectival phrases: 他 所 有 的 东 [東] 西 *tā sǔoyǒude dōngxi*: 'all his things'; 所 有 的 人 *sǔoyǒude rén*: 'all the people'. Another use, in 所 以 *sǔoyǐ*, matches this, since

以 *yǐ*: 'on account of' is already a relative idea; so *suǒyǐ* means 'all-that-on-account-of', or 'therefore': 我 很 忙, 所 以 不 能 再 来 [來] 了 *wǒ hěn máng, suǒyǐ bùnéng zài lái le*: 'I'm very busy, so can't come again'. For a real Western-type relative, one looks to *suǒ* in the pattern '*suǒ* plus active verb plus *de* plus object'; thus, 他 所 说 [說] 的 话 [話] 很 对 [對] *tā suǒ shuōde huà hěn dùi*: 'What he says is quite right'. Applied to a long phrase otherwise needing an awkward attributive, *suǒ* signals neatly: 我 把 你 所 借 的 东 [東] 西 都 拿 回 来 [來] 了 *wǒ bǎ nǐ suǒjiède dōngxi dōu náhuilaile*: ' I have taken back all those things which you borrowed' (replacing . . . *nǐ jiède nèixie dōngxi* . . . as the attributive). However, *suǒ* cannot refer back to a whole verbal clause except as *suǒyǐ*, and at most it avoids only marginal clumsiness.

Another means, 其 *qí*, also has literary antecedents. Originally it meant 'that (thing)', somewhat like a third-person indicator. Today, following a noun and joined to another element, it keeps its old force referring back to that noun and on to the joined element. Thus 其 他 *qítā* means 'the other, the remaining'; 其 中 *qízhōng* ('that-among') means 'among which'; 其 余 [餘] *qíyú*: 'the remainder of which'; 其 所 以 *qísuǒyǐ*: 'the reason thereof'; and 尤 其 是 *yóuqishi*: 'all the more'.

One more relative particle has also come down from *wényán*: 之 *zhī* showing the genitive somewhat as does *de*, and found in 'five per cent' (百 份 之 五 *bǎi fèn zhi wǔ*: hundred-parts-*zhi*-five'), and at the end of other statements involving one item among several. Thus, 'Chinese is one of the things which I am particularly interested in' becomes 'Chinese-is-my-*sǔo*-particularly-interested-things-*zhi*-one'.

Other situations needing a relative rely on long attributes, on the flexibility of verbs (see *Passives*), and on prepositional phrases following the item referred to (often formed on 以 *yǐ*).

Chinese acknowledges its own weakness here with the expression *yòng shǒuzhítou kàn* 'to read with the finger'. This is what happens when the reader struggles with modern Chinese prose which has tried to match the long encapsulations of Western languages: only by pointing off clauses and phrases, and sorting out subordinate from main, can he follow the passage. It is a weakness which has disturbed China's linguists since the nineteenth century, but no solution yet found can meet the linguistic need while respecting good Chinese style. The adoption of *bái huà* presupposes a solution acceptable to both speaking and writing. As the few means just discussed are used primarily in writing – educated people might occasionally speak them – the answer is probably still some way off.

Passives

Western verbs are generally visible at once as either passive or active. This formal distinction stays, even though often the passive simply marks a change of emphasis.

Chinese verbs, however, generally have an identical active and passive voice without formal alteration. There is furthermore little call for passives of mere emphasis. Thus, even the commonest verbs (to make, do, buy, read, etc.) express active and passive in their unaltered form. 他 看 书 [書] *tā kàn shū*: 'He is reading', and 书 [書] 都 看 完 了 *shū dōu kànwánle*: 'The books have all been read' do not differ formally. Also, verbs which in English have an impersonal passive use ('All the points have been noted', 'He is not considered reliable') translate actively into Chinese, leaving the agent unexpressed ('noted/considered by whom?').

Dual-voice verbs, like 'to smell' and 'to cook', are rare in English and somewhat idiomatic: 'That smells good – what's cooking?'. In Chinese this is entirely normal and uncolloquial. There is also no need to make distinctions such as between 'He was hanged this morning' and 'The picture hung on the wall', since most Chinese verbs resemble 'hang' in having such different senses. Edges of meaning, generally sharpened by different *verbs* in the Western languages, keep to one basic verb in Chinese and are marked in other ways. Thus, 'After he resigned' differs from 'After they sacked him' only by one added element, not by a change of basic verb. Likewise 死 *sǐ*: 'to die' is the same as in 打 死 *dǎsǐ*: 'to beat to death', or 'kill'. With such flexibility one might wonder if Chinese has a genuine passive, and how it could be used.

A number of directly transitive 'causative verbs' in Chinese as in English are counterparts to intransitives: 'to slay' as against 'to die'. The Chinese passive seems to have begun with these. Instead of the weak use of intransitive-plus-agent, as in 'to die at the hands of' (one early example), the stronger causative would be used for 'to be slain by'. A passive would thus be kept normally for a decisive action mentioning both subject and agent.

Modern passive use has widened, as have the means of showing it. Originally these were the particle 之 *zhī* (see page 119), linking verb to agent. Later came two auxiliary verbs, 受 *shòu* and 被 *bèi*. These last originally had the meaning of 'to suffer', and well matched the contexts of violent experience. Today, of these three means only *bèi* remains, since *shòu* has been widened into a verb of more general use ('to receive, get' with a causative sense of 'to impart, bestow'), while *zhī* is kept for the semi-literary genitive (met under *Relatives*). *Bèi* following a subject-noun marks a passive experience: 他 被 我 打 了 *tā bèi wǒ dǎle*: 'He was beaten by me'. The agent need not be stated any more than in English; compare the above agent-example with 他 被 选 [選] 为 [為] 总 [總] 统 [統] *tā bèi xuǎnwei zǒngtǒng*: 'He was elected president'. An impersonal agent (in the last example presumably 'the electorate') may be expressed by 人 *rén*, the English '(some)one'.

Used thus, 我 们 [們] 被 人 欺 负 [負] 了
wǒmen bèi rén qīfùle means 'We've been imposed upon'
(by particular people, or the world in general).

Sometimes a passive voice is reinforced with 给 [給]
gěi: literally 'to give', but here a co-verb placed immediately before the main verb. This, however, is more
common in spoken than in written Chinese; again
usually in speech, *bèi* may be replaced by 让 [讓] *ràng*
or 叫 *jiào*. These two are not complete passive-forming
elements. They emphasize the agent, but cannot be used
if no agent is present. Thus, 书 [書] 让 [讓] 孩 子
给 [給] 撕 碎 了 *shū ràng háizi gei sīsùle* has more
the meaning of 'It was the child who tore up the book'
than of 'The book was torn up by the child'.

As a distinct form, therefore, the passive is very seldom visible. As an attitude of mind, it is expressed most
naturally by the dual-voice quality of basic verbs. Countless Western passive constructions simply do not exist as
such in Chinese. They are actives, thought actively and
not merely expressed in that way. The only area for
which a passive will definitely be sought, outside of a
violent context, is that of a slightly sinister or unpleasant
outcome. So a passive fits 这 [這] 张 [張] 画 [畫]
被 他 画 [畫] 坏 [壞] 了 *zhèizhāng huàr bèi tā huà-
huàile*: 'This picture was spoilt ('painted-bad') by him',
but not . . . *bèi tā huàhǎole* ('painted-well').

Peking now seems to use *bèi* more frequently, perhaps in an attempt to spread the syntactic load over such
formal aids as do exist. The student should use *bèi* only

in the circumstances given above, though when translating from Chinese he must watch for active constructions which sound more natural as English passives.

Resultatives

The verb as a magnet attracting other elements is a fair summary of it as seen thus far. Verb-object compounds give the language much of its earthiness; the suffixes *lái* and *qù* show its attention to the point of interest; the aspect suffixes *-le* (*liǎo*) and *-zhe* (*zháo*) give finality importance over time.

A language built, like Chinese, on the additive principle seems well matched to the irrational and random nature of much of human life, since separate elements reordered to fit each new situation seem more 'like life' than do more regular and predictable patterns. Chinese brilliantly meets these expectations. The meaning of a compound verb may be both final and vague in effect. It may leave more room for manoeuvring than does that of a Western verb. The compound may also dispense with clumsy padding-out by auxiliaries detached from the main action, and thus better convey the speaker's true sense. But – the West expects to be told something, preferably 'the facts'; knowing that facts depend on their expression, Chinese believes the viewpoint onto them to be more significant. The ways in which these verbal compounds operate are a vital part of language and thought.

One type of compound verb gives a sense of result to its first element. Pidgin English 'to have a look-see', or closer inspection, is modelled on this. In Chinese the pattern links the neutral root-verb *kàn*: 'to look' with its more specific complement *jiàn*: 'to perceive', forming a compound, 看 见 [見] *kànjian*: 'to look at something and see it'. 见 [見] *jiàn*, though it may stand alone, is more usually linked with verbs of sense-perception (hear, see, smell) to give a resultative meaning. Such compounds belong together rather as do verb-object compounds, producing a single idea differing lexically from its parts.

Other verbal compounds, also expressing multiple ideas in one word, are not resultatives; e.g. 听 [聽] 说 [說] *tīngshuō*: 'to have heard (it) said'. It is not the *result* of the hearing (*tīng*) that is covered by the second element (*shuō*: 'to say'), nor does 'to say' give an extra focus to its first element. The two come together from two directions rather than from any inner logic.

Logical compounds of the *kànjian* type need not name an object. 我 看 见 [見] 了 *wǒ kànjianle*: 'I saw (it)'. Many of these resultatives give complex ideas requiring more than one English verb in translation. Their second element may be such suffixes as: 懂 *-dǒng*: 'to understand' (as in *kàndǒng*: 'to read and grasp', or 'to follow'); 开 [開] *-kāi*: 'to get open' (*bǎ mén dǎkāi*: 'to open the door'); 着 *-zháo*: 'to manage to'; 好 *-hǎo*: 'to complete satisfactorily'; 了

-*liǎo* and 完 -*wán*: 'to end, stop, run out'. They may be used literally with active verbs, but metaphorically they have wider uses, as has the co-verb of motion *dào* in 他 没 想 到 *tā méixiǎngdào*: 'He-think-not-arrive' for 'He didn't expect . . .'. Two more suffixes have a particular role in metaphor: 起 *qǐ*: 'to rise' and 住 *zhù*: 'to retain'. These are found in such contexts as 我 买 [買] 不 起 那 些 东 [東] 西 *wǒ mǎi-buqǐ nèixie dōngxi*: 'I buy-not-rise (i.e. cannot afford) those things', and 我 记 [記] 不 住 那 个 [個] 问 [問] 题 *wǒ jìbuzhù nèige wèntí*: 'I can't keep that problem in my mind (in-remembering-not-retain)'.

Although all these patterns are resultatives, two different types separate out within them: the actual and the potential. These distinguish verb-situations which are real (that is, have already occurred or are now doing so) from those which are speculative (in present or future terms of possibility). Before going into this, one must understand an element common to both types, the verb 得 *děi*.

Used alone, this is the optative verb 'ought to'. 你 得 去 *nǐ děi qù*: 'You ought to go'. Suffixed to another single verb of strong active sense, it matches the English '-able': 这 [這] 个 [個] 瓜 吃 得 *zhèige guā chīde*: 'This melon is eatable' (note that the pronunciation of 得 *děi* has weakened to *de*, and that this suffix use already approximates to a 'potential' sense of 'that which can be done').

Inserted into a verb compound, *děi* or *de* becomes a

weightless element, like a particle, covering potentiality or ability. Thus, 那 个 [個] 歌 儿 [兒] 你 唱 得 好 吗 [嗎]? *nèige gēr nǐ chàngdehǎo ma?* asks whether you can sing that song successfully, with *chàng*: 'to sing' as the root-verb and *-hǎo* as the resultative complement for 'successful conclusions'. A negative answer to the question goes 我 唱 不 好 *wǒ chàngbuhǎo*, and replaces *de* with *bu* ('not') in this potential pattern. Combinations of this type are virtually without number. Verb compounds with three or more elements, such as 想 起 来 [來] *xiǎngqǐlái*: 'think-rise-come' or 'to remember', may likewise take *de* or *bu* within them. There is nothing clumsy about the choice-type question 你 想 得 起 来 [來] 想 不 起 来 [來]? *nǐ xiǎngdeqilai xiǎngbuqilai?* for 'Can you remember?'. If one is at a loss for a translation with such weighty verbs, it may help to think of *de* (or *bu*) as 'in . . . (not)', referring to the first element of the compound. 看 得 见 [見] *kàndejiàn* will then be 'in seeing, perceive' as a step towards the translation as 'make out', with 看 不 见 [見] *kànbujiàn* in the same way becoming 'cannot make out'.

Thus far the potential type of resultative. The actual type is used for an act that is or is not coming about in reality, or did or did not happen in the past. Some examples: 我 要 学 [學] 好 中 文 *wǒ yào xué-hǎo zhōngwén*: 'I'm going to master Chinese' (study to a successful conclusion); 他 把 那 个 [個] 歌 儿 [兒] 唱 完 了 *tā bǎ nèige gēr chàngwánle*:

'He finished (sang-ended) that song'; 昨 天 你 没 看 见 [見] 他 吗 [嗎]? *zuótian nǐ méikànjian tā ma?*: 'Didn't you see him yesterday?' (*bu*: 'not' becoming *méi* in past situations). With these, there is no sense of speculation as to possibility. Either you did or did not see him; the song is over; the mastery of Chinese has begun. (Past possibility, as in 'Couldn't you see him?', takes auxiliary verbs and so is irrelevant here.)

For all this, 得 *de* may still be found with actual-type resultative compounds, at first sight in a manner resembling a potential use. This is quite illusory. For example, 他 念 书 [書]·念 得 快 *tā niànshū, niànde kuài* states that he is quick at studying, not speculating as to whether, if he studies, he will do so quickly or not. 快 *kuài* is adverbial, not a verb complement. The illusion may be even stronger in (say) 你·唱 得 好 *nǐ chàngde hǎo*, an actual-type sentence meaning 'Your singing is good', since in this case *hǎo* happens to be a verb complement as well as an adjective, and the whole phrase may appear to be of the potential type. However, the actual-type form in the negative (你 唱 得 不 好 *nǐ chàngde bùhǎo*: 'Your singing isn't good') clears the confusion by being immediately distinguishable from the potential negative *nǐ chàngbuhǎo*: 'You'll never get through that song'. Such overlaps make the use of *de* tricky at first. Matters are not helped by the script-mistake of some Chinese who write the adjectival *de* (的) instead of the correct 得 form in these 'actual' contexts.

This swing between reality and potentiality, on the axis of a single root-verb, makes a pattern flexible enough to cover an entire Western phrase or sentence. One such pattern will illustrate this: that formed on 起 *qǐ*: 'to rise'. Its basic use is as motion-verb: 起 来 [來] *qǐlái*: 'to get up', 站 起 来 [來] *zhànqǐlai*: 'to stand up'. Used with *-lái* it may also give an idea of 'starting to do something': 你 为 [為] 什 [甚] 么 [麼] 哭 起 来 [來] 了? *nǐ wèishénma kūqilaile?*: 'Why are you crying?', or less literally the two verbs may figure in 看 起 来 [來] *kànqilai*: 'to judge from appearances'. In the potential-type of resultative, *qǐ* may become the final complement, for example in the phrase for 'Excuse me' (对 [對] 不 起 *dùibuqi*: literally 'face-not-up'). Here an idiom, this may also be a genuine transitive verb meaning 'to dishonour, do wrong to': 他 对 [對] 不 起 中 国 [國] 人 *tā dùibuqi zhōngguo rén*: 'He has wronged the Chinese people' might be said of an erring politician. Similar is 看 不 起 *kànbuqi*: 'to despise', which also has a positive sense as in 他 很 看 得 起 我 *tā hěn kàndeqi wǒ*: 'He does me great honour'. Then the verb 买 [買] 不 起 *mǎibuqi* shows that 'one cannot buy' something (because its price is beyond one's means rather than because it is not available in the shops, which would use 买 [買] 不 着 *mǎibuzháo*). Another suggestion of impossibility is 作 不 起 来 [來] *zuòbuqǐlái*: 'not to get something done in the time', found in 衣 服 星 期 二 作 不 起 来 [來]

yīfu xīngqī èr zuòbuqilái: 'The clothes won't be ready by Tuesday'.

The above are only a few of the ways in which *qǐ* may form its pattern, and *qǐ* is only one of the elements available. The examples do, however, show that the Chinese verb is a flexible and expressive instrument – perhaps the language's finest single feature.

Some questions for Mr Li

7

The various sections of chapter 6 explain points of function and syntax as these are seen through Western eyes. This of course is not how the language appears to a Chinese. The following replies from an imaginary Chinese may come close to that, and may also give the casual reader something to take away with him.

Q There are no parts of speech in Chinese – how can you say exactly what you mean?

A Again the old confusion between script and speech. This is true only of a small part of our literary language, and in spoken Chinese there is no danger of mistaking a noun for a verb. Granted, certain categories (prepositions and verbs in particular) share something of each other's tasks, and that in general fewer distinct speech-parts are needed.

Q Chinese has no number-distinctions in its nouns and verbs, nor gender-distinctions in its personal pronouns – this must make for misunderstandings?

A It is easier to be specific if you start from an unemphatic level and have the choice of being neutral or not. To say 'Book I want, newspaper I don't' may be more accurate when it is not 'a book (in general)' or 'those newspapers (in particular)'; both halves of the sentence share the same neutrality. And when actually counting things we have suffixes to put onto numerals which help to emphasize them: 'four volumes' instead of just 'four (books)'. With 'he' and 'she', we prefer to name or identify the person: 'wife tells him', if need be. You, after all, make no distinction of sex with 'they'. In Chinese number and gender, there are more 'they' categories of a neutral type and more freedom of choice to be either neutral or specific in the means available.

Q A Chinese sentence seems utterly without internal plan.

A This is because of two things in particular: the relation of subject to predicate, and the directional way in which syntax operates. Thus, on the first point, the subject may be the entire topic, or something over and above the topic which is implied, and the predicate some small drop of comment or of attitude towards it which may not be an action or attribute of the subject. 'My wife cannot cook – very good' may be saying 'It's fine that my wife can't cook, since this gives us the excuse to eat out', but only a tiny catch in the breath (shown here by the dash) marks off predicate from subject (often as here itself subject and predicate). On direction, 'The children have had enough to eat' is literally the same phrase as 'Children? I don't want to have any more of them'. True, the verb-idiom differs and there is a catch of breath again for the second sense, but a much more important matter is the difference in viewpoint, which supplies a new subject ('I') and a new direction back on to a pre-stated topic. The logic of a Chinese sentence centres on its point of interest.

Q Time is not built in to the Chinese verb with tenses – how can it express all the nuances of prospective or retrospective action?

A Like Western languages, Chinese uses auxiliaries but makes them do other things. Most usually, the auxiliary deals with *finality* of action, at whatever time, and this is the only verbal time-idea that cannot be expressed by adverbs (when absolute) or context (when relative). This finality aspect allows some notions involving time to be given if anything a better deal than they get in Western languages. When we say 'It's going to rain' or 'Let's be off!' the form is that of actions already begun and beyond recall, whereas for you that is only the implied sense. Finality can operate independently of time, as everyone knows who has felt time catch up with events. Our verb can also express *result*. The effect is something like your perfective: 'to look' may be 'to perceive'. Again, as with number, a neutral category is open if no such nuance is required.

Texts

8

The first text set out on the next page is a poem by Jǐa Dǎo (779–843) of the Tang dynasty, and is entitled 'Looking for a hermit and not meeting him' (*xún yǐnzhě búyù*). Shown alongside each character are the entries which might be given for it in a small Chinese–English dictionary.

The poem's twenty characters have upwards of eighty quite distinct meanings when examined individually in this way: does this imply that an approach to its total meaning has only a one-in-four chance of success? Obviously not. A closer look will show that to give correct context-meanings to the characters is not difficult, nor indeed the main item in appreciating what by classical Chinese standards is quite an easy poem. Its real difficulties lie elsewhere. And they would remain as the crux of appreciation even if glossing the poem were to require an algebraical substitution for the characters one by one – and things are not quite so bad.

Hollow dots mark off four lines in column.

松	sōng	pine, fir-tree
下	xià	to descend, fall; to begin (work); below; under, inside; deprecatory phrase used of oneself when addressing superiors
問	wèn	to ask, inquire, investigate; to send; to hold responsible; to require from
童	tóng	lad, youth; bare, undefiled
子。	zǐ	son; 'you' in direct address; 'the Master' (i.e. Confucius); seed; noun-forming suffix
言	yán	words, speech; to talk, express, mean
師	shī	teacher, instructor; to imitate; an army
採	cǎi	to pluck, choose, gather, collect
藥	yào	drugs, healing herbs; to administer drugs
去。	qù	to go away; past, gone; to remove, get rid of
只	zhǐ	merely, only; but, yet
在	zài	at, in, on; to rest with, consist in; alive, be present; with reference to, in the case of
此	cǐ	this, here
山	shān	hill, mountain; a grave
中	zhōng	middle; among, within, between, in; China, Chinese; (fourth tone) to hit in the centre, attain; to fancy; to fall into a trap
。		
雲	yún	clouds, cloudy; numerous; to gather
深	shēn	deep, profound; abstruse; very, extremely
不	bù	negative prefix
知	zhī	to know, perceive; (fourth tone) wisdom
處	chù	place, office; department; condition, circumstances; (third tone) to dwell, abide in, occupy; to decide, punish, settle; to manage, adjust.
。		

Clearing the ground, one assumes from the title that some person is or was hoping to meet the hermit. The subject therefore cannot be 'pine tree', nor (to go by the order of 'subject-verb-object') is it 'youth'. This suggests a 'supplied' subject, most probably 'I' or 'we', since Chinese poetry deals in general with first-person feelings and observations. In that case, 'pine tree' cannot govern *xià*, in the latter's verbal senses, but must be combining with it in a place-where phrase: 'under the pine'. So the first five characters may be read as 'Under the pine tree (I) ask the youth(s)'. 'To ask' is very much the basic meaning of *wèn*, the others given for it being relatively rare and found only in compounds. The plural-forming suffix *-men* is a *bái huà* feature not used in classical Chinese, so its absence from after *tóngzǐ* is not significant: there may or may not be one, or more than one, youth.

The five following characters soon emerge as meaning '(He) says teacher go/gone to gather herbs' ('to collect medicines', as though from a dispensary, would not be a likely reading). Similarly, the next five: 'Only in the mountain' (*zài*: 'here' is not a strong place-word, and *zhōng* therefore carries the weight of 'in' or 'among', referring back to *shān*). The final five characters may be read 'Clouds thick, not know place'.

If the dictionary has taken one that far, it is tempting to begin a complete translation, perhaps along these lines: 'Under the pine tree I ask the youth/He says "My master has gone to gather simples/He is only a little way off in the mountain/But the clouds are thick and I do not know the spot" '. However, the art of Chinese poetry, as of its landscape painting, is to suggest rather than to make statements. What is suggested may be both precise and vague. The tentative English translation has precision, but it is of the wrong kind; where the original rests on its lack of single, specific meanings for its effect, the English is cut-and-dried.

The Chinese poem leaves room for doubt on many counts. To begin with, who is 'under the pine tree'? The questioner has climbed halfway up a mountain, and might wish for a rest in the shade. Alternatively, the youth might be waiting there for him to come up; or both of them might be standing there. Then, how many trees are involved – one, or a whole grove? What is the relationship of 'master' to 'youth'? Is the boy merely a servant, or (more likely) is he a disciple or pupil? But, if he is studying Taoist ways with the hermit, as a pupil, then why has he not gone with him to collect the herbs? He may after all be a servant. Next, the meaning of 'only'. Is it 'merely', in terms of the distance the master has gone, or 'all that I know', as said by the youth of the whole situation? How many mountains are there? Is the action set amidst a ring of them, or on one alone? Lastly, the final five characters: are these a disclaimer spoken by the youth, or a justification made by the visitor of his wasted visit? And does *yún shēn* mean 'cloud (is) thick', or '(He is in) the midst of the cloud' – said of the hermit?

Such questions are as real for a Chinese as for a foreign reader. They form part of the meaning of the poem and of its own kind of vagueness. In other more complex classical texts there will be even more latitude in the reading of certain characters, and at times much disagreement among commentators as to how they should be understood. Social habits change, and with them the shorthand allusions to customs familiar at the time but now obscure. There may be references to mythology, and cryptic images quite outside the readers' experience may be present, all of which will make a literal translation less easy than that attempted here. Yet the work demanded after such understanding has been reached does not much alter from text to text.

*

The passage facing is from a speech by Máo Tsé-tūng given at Yenan, North China, in 1942. Its characters here are drawn simplified, although Chairman Mao's utterances often appear in the old 'regular' characters.

Over 1,000 years separate this passage and the 'Hermit' poem by Jǐa Dǎo, about the same interval of time as that between a wartime speech by Churchill and the Anglo-Saxon *Beowulf*. Yet the Chinese poem can today be read by anyone familiar with its characters.

What are the main differences that may be noted in these two texts? First, a change of medium. Mao was speaking to an audience, and so had to be followed by

我们还要学习古人语言中有
生命的东西。由於我们没有
努力学习语言，古人语言中
的许多还有生气的东西我们
就没有充分的合理的利用。
当然我们坚决反对去用已经
死了的语彙和典故，这是确
定了的，但是好的仍然有用
的东西还是应该继承。

*Wǒmen hái yào xuéxí gǔrén yǔyán zhōng yǒu shēngmìng-
de dōngxi. Yóuyu wǒmen méiyou nǔlì xuéxí yǔyán, gǔrén
yǔyán zhōngde xǔduō hái yǒu shēngqìde dōngxi wǒmen
jiù méiyou chōngfēnde hélǐde lìyong. Dāngrán wǒmen
jiānjué fǎndùi qù yòng yǐjing sǐlede yǔhùi hé diǎngù,
zhèi shi quèdìnglede, dànshi hǎode réngrán yǒuyòngde
dōngxi háishi yīnggāi jìchéng.*

(We must also learn to adopt what is still alive in the
language of the ancients. Because we have not exerted
ourselves to learn language, we have not made full
and reasonable use of much that is still alive in the
ancient language. It goes without saying that we are
resolutely opposed to the use of expressions or classical
allusions that are already dead, but what is good and
useful should be taken over.)

[139]

ear rather than by eye. His speech thus has eleven 'formal' syllables (or more than 10 per cent) making for aural understanding; the poem has only one (the *zǐ* of *tóngzǐ*). This illustrates a main feature of colloquial Chinese as against the literary style (see page 73 and elsewhere). Understanding by ear is further reinforced by the structure of compounds in Mao: there are a dozen which are made up of similarities, both halves matching in meaning (see page 66). Among these are *xúexí*: 'study-practise', *qùedìng*: 'sure-definite', *yīnggāi*: 'should-ought'. Then there are filler-words, somewhat like English conjunctions, which belong to speech as a means of carrying the listener from one idea to another: *jìu*: 'thus', *dāngrán*: 'of course', *dànshi*: 'but'. All these are *bái huà* features.

Secondly, there is far more clarity of meaning in Mao. Gone are the vague strokes of a landscape painting such as characterized the poem. Immediately it is plain who is the subject: *wǒmen*: 'we' – and this is no editorial 'we', but refers to actual party workers present at the time. Note also how the particle *de* is used to help signal adjectives, past participles, and adverbs.

Thirdly, one notices expressions modelled on the Japanese (see page 69), such as *chōngfēn*: 'full', *fǎndùi*: 'to oppose', and *lìyong*: 'use', which were consciously taken up by modernists in China as a means of widening vocabulary.

Fourthly, the passage illustrates many of the syntax points discussed in chapter 6. Among these are: postpositional adjectives to make prepositions, as *zhōng* here for 'among'; pre-statement of the object, here a splendid example which runs from after the first comma down to *dōngxi*; and the extended use of the directional verb *qù* for something more than 'to go'.

For all these differences and changes, Chairman Mao's general point of substance is one that can be observed from study of the two texts together. China's past is indeed not easily separated from her present and future.

The hundred radicals listed here (and see page 48) all have basic meanings in themselves (though some will only be 'free' words in literary Chinese – for example, radical 124 *yǔ* normally takes -*máo* as its second element for 'feathers').

But they are not the only radicals which may be said to have basic meanings. Others (not included in the list) such as 189 *gāo*: 'tall', 168 *cháng*: 'long', 201 *huáng*: 'yellow', are indeed more common than some of the listed characters, such as the archaic 73 *yūe*: 'to say', or the obsolescent term for 'an official': 131 *chén*. The explanation for these appearing at the expense of others individually more deserving concerns their usefulness *as radicals*. There seems little to be gained from learning, say, 183 *fēi*: 'to fly' as a radical, since for practical writing purposes it never appears as one, but only as a character in its own right; it is therefore omitted. Conversely, although there might seem to be more valuable single characters than 198 *lù*: 'deer', it is the radical in about twenty other characters, and so has earned its place. The list, in short, tries to balance usefulness as a separate character against frequency as a radical. For this reason, a round number of one hundred has been taken to avoid the implication that the listing is final and inclusive.

Note that the characters are written in their 'regular' forms, and not in their communist simplifications. The latter are still used somewhat inconsistently by Peking, with a tendency for radicals to persist in their full forms, especially when found as separate characters. (See also chapter 11.)

1	一	*yī*	one
7	二	*èr*	two
9	人, 亻	*rén*	man
11	入	*rù*	to enter
12	八	*bā*	eight
18	刀, 刂	*dāo*	knife
19	力	*lì*	strength
24	十	*shí*	ten
29	又	*yòu*	also, again
30	口	*kǒu*	mouth
32	土	*tǔ*	earth
33	士	*shì*	scholar
37	大	*dà*	big
38	女	*nǔ*	woman
39	子	*zǐ*	son
41	寸	*cùn*	inch
42	小	*xiǎo*	little
44	尸	*shī*	corpse
46	山	*shān*	mountain

47	川	*chuān*	river
48	工	*gōng*	work
49	己	*jǐ*	self
61	心, 忄	*xīn*	heart
63	户	*hù*	door
64	手, 扌	*shǒu*	hand
67	文	*wén*	literature
69	斤	*jīn*	catty
70	方	*fāng*	square
72	日	*rì*	sun
73	曰	*yūe*	to say
74	月	*yuè*	moon
75	木	*mù*	tree
81	比	*bǐ*	to compare
82	毛	*máo*	hair
85	水, 氵	*shuǐ*	water
86	火, 灬	*huǒ*	fire
88	父	*fù*	father
91	片	*piàn*	slice
93	牛, 牜	*niú*	cow
96	玉, 王	*yù*	jade
97	瓜	*gūa*	melon
100	生	*shēng*	to be born
101	用	*yòng*	to use
102	田	*tián*	field
103	匹	*pǐ*	bolt of cloth
106	白	*bái*	white
107	皮	*pí*	skin

109	目, 目	*mù*	eye
112	石	*shí*	stone
117	立	*lì*	to stand
118	竹	*zhú*	bamboo
119	米	*mǐ*	rice
123	羊	*yáng*	sheep
124	羽	*yǔ*	feather, wing
125	老	*lǎo*	old
126	而	*ér*	and (yet)
128	耳, 耳	*ěr*	ear
130	肉, 月	*ròu*	flesh
131	臣	*chén*	official
132	自	*zì*	self
135	舌	*shé*	tongue
139	色	*sè*	colour
143	血	*xùe*	blood
144	行	*xíng*	to go
145	衣, 衤	*yī*	clothing
146	西	*xī*	west
147	見	*jiàn*	to see
148	角	*jiǎo*	horn
149	言	*yán*	speech
151	豆	*dòu*	bean
156	走	*zǒu*	to walk
157	足	*zú*	foot
158	身	*shēn*	body
159	車	*chē*	vehicle
160	辛	*xīn*	bitter

166	里	lǐ	mile
167	金	jīn	metal, gold
169	門	mén	gate
173	雨	yǔ	rain
174	青	qīng	green
175	非	fēi	not
177	革	gé	raw skin
180	音	yīn	sound
181	頁	yè	page
182	風	fēng	wind
184	食	shí	food
186	香	xiāng	fragrance
187	馬	mǎ	horse
188	骨	gǔ	bone
194	鬼	guǐ	demon
195	魚	yú	fish
196	鳥	niǎo	bird
198	鹿	lù	deer
199	麥	mài	wheat
200	麻	má	hemp
202	黍	shǔ	millet
203	黑	hēi	black
207	鼓	gǔ	drum
209	鼻	bí	nose
212	龍	lóng	dragon

The following compounds are some of those which may
be formed by taking characters from the 'hundred radi-

cals' list and placing them together. As words, they have no special merits to give them priority in being learnt; as mnemonics for remembering the radicals, however, they are a useful first guide to consulting a Chinese dictionary.

1/74	一 月	*yíyuè*	January
1/158	一 身	*yìshēn*	the whole body
7/74	二 月	*èryuè*	February
9/19/159	人 力 車	*rénlìchē*	rickshaw
9/30	人 口	*rénkǒu*	population
11/32	入 土	*rùtǔ*	to inter
11/64	入 手	*rùshǒu*	elementary
12/74	八 月	*bāyuè*	August
18/91	刀 片	*dāopiàn*	razor blade
24/7/74	十 二 月	*shíèryuè*	December
24/74	十 月	*shíyuè*	October
24/157	十 足	*shízú*	complete
30/180	口 音	*kǒuyīn*	pronunciation
32/9	土 人	*tǔrén*	native, local man
32/182	土 風	*tǔfēng*	local custom
37/42	大 小	*dàxiǎo*	size
37/145	大 衣	*dàyī*	overcoat
37/169	大 門	*dàmén*	front door, main gate
37/182	大 風	*dàfēng*	typhoon
37/199	大 麥	*dàmài*	barley
38/9	女 人	*nǚrén*	woman
42/61	小 心	*xiǎoxīn*	to take care
42/119	小 米	*xiǎomǐ*	yellow millet

42/123	小 羊	xiǎoyáng	lamb
42/199	小 麥	xiǎomài	wheat
46/85	山 水	shānshuǐ	scenery
46/123	山 羊	shānyáng	goat
46/146	山 西	Shānxī	Shansi province
48/9	工 人	gōngrén	worker
64/48	手 工	shǒugōng	handicrafts
64/61	手 心	shǒuxīn	palm of the hand
67/149	文 言	wényán	literary style
70/41	方 寸	fāngcùn	square inch (fig. heart)
70/149	方 言	fāngyán	local dialect
70/166	方 里	fānglǐ	square mile
72/101	日 用	rìyòng	everyday use
75/48	木 工	mùgōng	carpent/ry, -er
81/70	比 方	bǐfāng	example
82/107	毛 皮	máopí	fur
82/145	毛 衣	máoyī	sweater
85/19	水 力	shuǐlì	water-power
85/93	水 牛	shuǐníu	water-buffalo
85/196	水 鳥	shuǐniǎo	aquatic bird
86/46	火 山	huǒshān	volcano
86/159	火 車	huǒchē	railway train
93/130	牛 肉	níuròu	beef
96/119	玉 米	yùmǐ	maize
96/139	玉 色	yùsè	jade-coloured
100/9	生 人	shēngrén	stranger

[148]

100/72	生 日	shēngrì	birthday
106/72	白 日	báirì	daytime
106/167	白 金	báijīn	platinum
107/82	皮 毛	pímáo	superficial
107/177	皮 革	pígé	leather
123/82	羊 毛	yángmáo	sheepswool
123/130	羊 肉	yángròu	mutton
124/82	羽 毛	yǔmáo	feathers
125/39	老 子	lǎozǐ	Lao-tse, the philosopher
125/64	老 手	lǎoshǒu	old hand
130/91	肉 片	ròupiàn	slices of meat
132/37	自 大	zìdà	conceited
132/49	自 己	zìjǐ	oneself
132/117	自 立	zìlì	independ/ence, -ent
132/144/159	自行車	zìxíngchē	bicycle
132/157	自 足	zìzú	pleased with oneself
146/70	西 方	xīfāng	'the West'
146/97	西 瓜	xīgūa	watermelon
169/30	門 口	ménkǒu	entrance
173/145	雨 衣	yǔyī	raincoat
182/85	風 水	fēngshǔi	geomancy (study of natural sites and their influences)
186/85	香 水	xiāngshǔi	perfume
187/19	馬 力	mǎlì	horsepower
195/39	魚 子	yúzǐ	fish roe
203/9	黑 人	hēirén	Negro
207/64	鼓 手	gǔshǒu	drummer

Writing

Even if one wished only to read Chinese and never write the characters, one would still need to know the stroke-principles governing them and (see page 45) their ordering in a dictionary. What constitutes a stroke in writing Chinese is seen by studying the first twelve characters below: the strokes are numbered in sequence and the arrows inside the strokes show the direction to be followed by brush or pen; page-references are to the character's first appearance in the book.

dōng: east (page 37)

dūo: much, many (page 44)

men: (plural suffix) (page 82)

dōu: all (page 83)

 xie: (plural suffix)

 wǒ: I, me (page 85)

 kàn: to look (page 86)

 yě: both . . . and; also (page 94)

 huà: speech, language (page 95)

 měi: each, every (page 99)

 yīng: Eng-(lish) (page 100)

 jīng: in 'already' (page 112)

[151]

About Chinese

The sequence of strokes, as distinct from the direction in which they are made, may need more attention. Below, written in pattern style with an ordinary ball-point pen, are fifty characters taken from chapter 6 ('regular' forms are here given before 'simplified').

來　　(一 ⼆ ⺊ ⽊ ⽊ 朿 求 來)

[来]　(一 ⺊ ⼄ 三 ⺗ 来 来)

　　　lái: to come (page 83)

他 亻　(丿 亻)

　也　(⼄ 力 也)

　　　tā: he, him

不　　(一 丆 万 不)

　　　bu: (negative prefix)

那　　(⼄ 刀 尹 尹 尹 ' 尹 ⼽ 那)

　　　nèi: that

好 女　(⼥ 女 女)

　子　(⺈ 了 子)

　　　hǎo: good

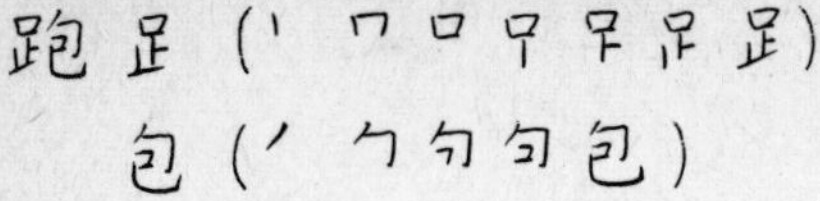

跑 足 (丿 �𠂆 口 尸 尸 吊 足)
  包 (丿 勹 勺 勺 包)

    pǎo: to run (page 85)

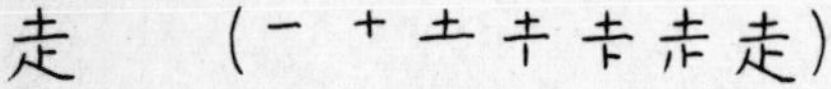

走 (一 十 土 キ 圥 夫 走)

    zǒu: to go, walk

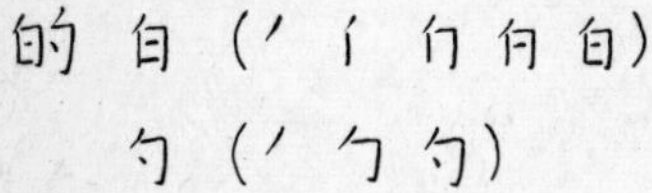

的 白 (丿 亻 亻 白 白)
  勺 (丿 勹 勺)

    de: (adjectival suffix) (page 86)

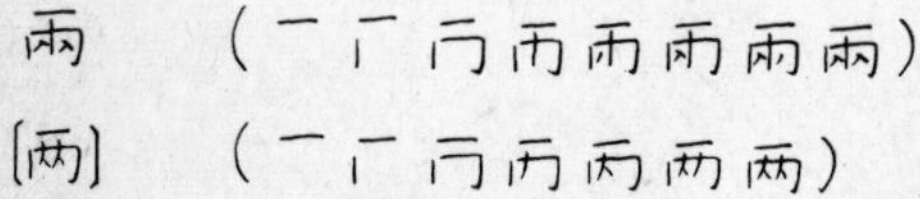

兩 (一 ⺄ 冂 兩 兩 兩 兩 兩)
[两] (一 ⺄ 冂 丙 丙 两 两)

    liǎng: two (page 88)

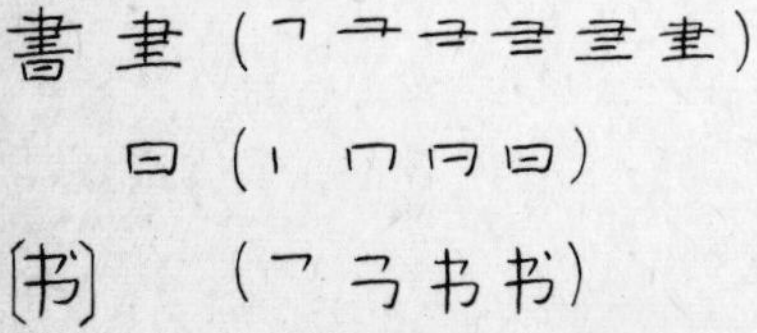

書 聿 (⁊ ⺕ 肀 聿 聿 聿)
  曰 (丨 冂 曰 曰)
[书] (⁊ 乛 书 书)

    shū: book (page 89)

飯 食 (ノ 人 人 今 今 今 食 食)

   反 (´ 厂 厅 反)

[饭] 饣 (´ 𠂊 饣)

   反 (´ 厂 厅 反)

     fàn: cooked rice (page 90)

萬 ⧾⧾ (一 十 ⧾ ⧾⧾)

   禺 (丨 冂 冂 日 旦 昌 禺 禺)

[万] (一 丁 万)

     wàn: ten thousand (page 91)

鋪 舍 (ノ 人 人 今 全 全 舍 舍)

   甫 (一 丁 万 万 甫 甫 甫)

     pù: shop

天 (一 二 于 天)

     tiān: day, heaven (page 92)

没 氵 (丶 冫 氵)

   殳 (丿 几 𠘧 殳)

     méi: (negative prefix)

[154]

像 亻 (ノ 亻)

　象 (ノ ク ケ タ 刍 缶 多 多 牟 多 象 象)

[象] (ノ ク ケ タ 刍 缶 多 多 牟 多 象 象)

xiàng: to resemble (page 93)

是 (丨 冂 冂 日 旦 早 早 是 是)

shì: to be

回 (丨 冂 冂 冂 回 回 回)

húi: to return

認 言 (丶 亠 亠 言 言 言 言)

　刃 (フ 刀 刃)

　心 (丶 心 心 心)

[认] 讠 (丶 亠 讠)

　人 (ノ 人)

rèn: to recognize

識 言 （ ` 二 二 亖 言 言 言 ）

　　立 （ ` 二 亠 六 立 ）

　　日 （ ｜ 冂 日 日 ）

　　戈 （ 一 弋 戈 戈 ）

[识] 讠 （ ` ㇇ 讠 ）

　　只 （ ｜ 冂 口 只 只 ）

　　　shì: to know; (in *rènshi*) to recognize (page 93)

道 首 （ ` ㇀ 丷 丷 产 首 首 首 ）

　　辶 （ ` 氵 辶

　　　dào: way; (in *zhīdao*) to know

聞 門 （ ｜ 冂 冂 冃 冃 門 門 門 ）

　　耳 （ 一 丁 Ｔ 丌 耳 耳 ）

[闻] 门 （ ` ｀ 门 ）

　　耳 （ 一 丁 Ｔ 丌 耳 耳 ）

　　　wén: to hear (page 94)

去 　　（ 一 十 土 去 去 ）

　　　qù: to go (page 96)

擊 軎 (一 厂 厂 币 而 虿 車 軎 軎)

　　殳 (丶 几 卪 殳)

　　手 (ノ 二 三 手)

[击] 　 (一 二 十 击 击)

　　　　jí: (in *gōngjī*) to attack (page 96)

睡 目 (丨 冂 冂 月 目)

　　垂 (ノ 二 二 千 千 禾 垂 垂 垂)

　　　　shùi: to sleep

覺 與 (ノ イ イ ʹ 白 臼 𦥑 𦥑 𦥑 𦥑 與 與)

　　見 (丨 冂 月 月 目 見 見)

[觉] 𫩏 (丶 丷 丷 ⺍ 𫩏)

　　见 (丨 冂 贝 见)

　　　　jiào: (in *shùijiào*) to sleep

戲 虛 (丶 ⺊ ⺊ 广 卢 卢 虍 虍 虖 虘 虘 虛 虛)

　　戈 (一 弋 戈 戈)

[戏] 又 (乛 又)

　　戈 (一 弋 戈 戈)

　　　　xì: play (page 98)

出　　（丨 十 屮 出 出）

chū: to come/go out (page 98)

中　　（丨 冂 口 中）

zhōng: China, Chinese (page 99)

國　口（丨 冂 口）
　　或（一 丁 亓 古 豆 或 或 或）

国　口（丨 冂 口）
　　玉（一 二 千 王 玉）

　　　gúo: country

聰　耳（一 丁 丌 开 耳 耳）
　　悤（丿 亻 冇 冇 匆 匈 悤）
　　心（丶 心 心 心）

聪　耳（一 丁 丌 开 耳 耳）
　　总（丶 丷 丷 总 总）
　　心（丶 心 心 心）

　　　cōng: clever (page 100)

明 日 （｜ 冂 円 日）

　　月 （丿 刀 月 月）

　　　míng: (in *cōngmíng*) clever (page 100)

飛 　（乁 乀 飞 乁 飛 飛 飛 飛 飛）

〔飞〕（乁 乁 飞）

　　　fēi: to fly (page 101)

機 木 （一 十 オ 木）

　　幾 （ㄠ ㄠ ㄠ ㄠˊ ㄠㄠ ㄠㄠ 丝 丝 丝 幾 幾 幾）

〔机〕木 （一 十 オ 木）

　　几 （丿 几）

　　　jī: machine

在 　（一 ナ オ 在 在 在）

　　　zài: in, at

北 　（｜ 十 킈 킈 北）

　　　běi: north

京 　（丶 亠 亠 古 亨 京 京）

　　　jīng: capital

今 　（丿 人 今 今）

　　　jīn: now

[159]

老 (一 十 土 耂 老 老)

lǎo: old (page 104)

縱 糸 (𠃋 幺 幺 糸 糸 糸)

從 (丿 彳 彳 彳 彳 從 從 從 從 從 從)

[纵] 纟 (𠃋 纟 纟)

从 (丿 人 从 从)

zòng: to relax (page 105)

響 鄉 (𠃋 幺 乡 乡 乡 乡 乡 乡 乡 乡 鄉 鄉)

音 (丶 亠 亠 立 立 音 音 音 音)

[响] 口 (丨 𠃍 口)

向 (丿 亻 门 向 向 向)

xiǎng: echo (page 106)

壞 土 (一 十 土)

褱 (丶 亠 亠 亠 亠 亠 亠 亠 亠 亠 亠 亠 亠

褱 褱 褱)

[坏] 土 (一 十 土)

不 (一 丆 不 不)

huài: bad (page 107)

邊 自 （ ＇ 亻 亻 仢 伯 自 ）

　　穿 （ ＇ ﾉ 宀 宀 宀 宁 空 空 穿 ）

　　辶 （ 丶 ㇋ 辶 ）

[边] 力 （ フ 力 ）

　　辶 （ 丶 ㇋ 辶 ）

　　　　bīan(r): side (page 109)

後 彳 （ ＇ ㇒ 彳 ）

　　夋 （ ㇂ 幺 幺 糹 夅 夋 ）

[后] 　 （ ＇ 广 厂 后 后 后 ）

　　　　hòu: back, behind (page 110)

還 睘 （ 丶 冂 罒 罒 罒 罒 睘 睘 晋 署 胃 睘 睘 ）

　　辶 （ 丶 ㇋ 辶 ）

[还] 不 （ 一 丆 不 不 ）

　　辶 （ 丶 ㇋ 辶 ）

　　　　hái: or (page 112)

點 黑 （ ＇ 冂 冂 冈 囚 里 里 黒 黒 黒 黑 黑 ）

　　占 （ 丨 十 卜 占 占 ）

[点] 占 （ 丨 十 卜 占 占 ）

　　灬 （ 丶 丷 灬 灬 ）

　　　　diǎn(r): little (page 113)

想 木 (一 十 才 木)

目 (丨 冂 冃 冃 目)

心 (丶 心 心 心)

    xiǎng: to plan to (page 114)

次 (丶 丶 冫 冸 次 次)

    cì: occasion, time

選 巴 (丆 コ 巴 巴 巴 巴)

共 (一 十 卄 井 共 共)

辶 (丶 彡 辶)

[选] 先 (丿 ㇒ 牛 生 失 先)

辶 (丶 彡 辶)

    xuǎn: to choose (page 122)

衣 (丶 亠 产 产 衣 衣)

    yī: clothing (page 129)

Simplification 11

Chinese in alphabetized form (*pīnyīn*) may be viewed as both a means of promoting a unified speech and of making it easier to write. Alphabetization thus touches on all the problems of stylistic reform which result when a language changes its medium. Simplification of retained ideographs does not itself reach so far. This is only a temporary measure, part of what the President of the Chinese Academy of Sciences has called 'the gradual fading-out' of the characters, and it leaves style and content unaffected.

The effects of simplified characters (aesthetics apart) are therefore open to exaggeration. Because they date from after 1949 and the communist takeover, the new characters are often attacked for reasons which belong more to politics than to linguistics. Within China, the attitude to them seems to be quite relaxed, and the visitor may notice frequent anomalies to confirm this. One such is at the very centre of Peking. The huge legend 'Long Live the Chinese People's Republic' which adorns one side of the Imperial palace is naturally written throughout in simplified characters, including

华 for the *huá* of *zhōnghuá* (the expression used for 'Chinese'). Yet scarcely a hundred yards away, an Office of Public Security building carries a plaque on which *huá* is in the old, 'regular' style 華 .

It should not be assumed from this that the introduction of the new script has been completely without problems. The cost must have been enormous, far greater than that (say) of introducing decimal coinage in Britain. By simplifying out some (but not all) of the radicals, the new characters have played havoc with catalogues, lists of all kinds, and works of reference, since the old system of 'radical plus stroke-count' has been made unworkable. One recent dictionary classifies alphabetically by *pīnyīn*, yet retains a radical index (for consulting a character of which the sound is not known) but on a new basis of 186 instead of 214 radicals. This may become standard, but until it does the old reference works will stay on the shelves. Then again, few as yet of China's teachers can have had all their own school education in the new script, and it is hard to imagine that those who were not thus educated can be completely confident in teaching the simplified characters. There are, moreover, some larger questions to be asked of its long-term practical advantages in education: it makes the characters look more alike (by reducing their strokes by an average of about fifty per cent) – but could they not thus become easier to confuse?

For all this, the new characters are not a problem to their Chinese users but a solution to a problem. They are only really difficult when one does not know much Chinese to begin with. A foreigner sees them as one more aspect of the language that must be rationalized before it is studied. This rationale, and the technique of simplified characters, may be given three main headings:

1. An existing character's use is widened to cover one or more homophones (a simplification in that older complex forms for such homophones are eliminated). By this, 里 *lǐ* as a simplified character (henceforth SC) stands for the former 裏 *lǐ*: 'inside' as well as for the 里 *lǐ* of 'mile'. Similarly 面 *miàn* now does duty for the former 麵 *miàn*: 'flour', as well as for the 面 *miàn* of 'face, side'. The earlier character for 'empress', 后 *hòu*, is made to stand also for the regular 後 *hòu*, meaning 'after, behind'. These widened uses are limited to a fairly small number of homophones with clearly distinguishable meanings; sometimes the tone varies from that of the original, but never the basic sound.

2. A reduction in the total strokes of a character is made, but its overall outline is kept or suggested. The gain in speed of writing is obvious. Although at times the reductions are arbitrary, they are made in four ways:

(a) by re-thinking the character (see the historical typology, pages 36–7). This may be done either associatively or phonetically: thus, 宝 *bǎo* replaces the complex 寶 *bǎo*: 'treasure' by placing 'jade' [玉] under 'roof' [宀], forming a perfect 'associative' ideograph.

Phonetically, 优 *yōu*: 'excellent' takes a sound-element for its right-hand part instead of the complex group in 優.

(b) by taking one element of the traditional form to stand for the whole SC. By this, 电 is used instead of 電 *diàn*: 'electricity', the top part (the 'rain' radical) being dropped. The element chosen may be inner or outer, top or bottom, left or right; thus, 開 *kāi*: 'to open' drops its 'door' radical and keeps only the inner part in its SC form 开.

(c) by cutting repeated elements, whereby 蟲 *chóng*: 'insect' becomes 虫 (in itself the 'insect' radical, so a harmless change). Sometimes *all* such elements may go, leaving unchanged only an outer shell, as in 断 *duàn*: 'to discontinue', for 斷. Other characters of this type reduce complex recurring to simple recurring elements, such as the upper part of 勞 *láo*: 'to labour', which becomes as in 劳.

(d) by taking certain recurring components and giving them stereotype-forms for use on all occasions when they would recur. One such example, the stereotype 又, is used interchangeably for each of the following five components: 蓳, 盧, 坙, 茣, and 奚. These five, chosen because they tended to occur in meaningfully remote two-part characters not likely to be confused, are now generally replaced by 又, so that for instance the character 難 *nán*: 'difficult' is given a SC-form 难. Another stereotype 不 replaces the components 睘 and 襄; thus, 还 is now written for 還 *hái*: 'or'.

Stereotypes are the neatest way of simplifying; unfortunately they are not always met when expected. Take the character above, *nán*, in its traditional form 難, and look at it in comparison with the traditional 進 *jìn*: 'to enter'. The component common to both is plainly 隹, and one might expect to see this cut or replaced in both characters in the same way. But it is not. With *jìn* it is the right-hand component which is reduced to make 进 for the SC; *nán*, however, applies a stereotype to its left-hand component, producing 难. Cases such as these can be troublesome. They discourage simplification by analogy; what is good for A may not apply to B.

3. A final simplification method must briefly be mentioned as being the most drastic of those so far attempted by Peking. This concerns the radicals and phonetics, a number of which now have fixed stereotypes (with one form unique to each, unlike the stereotypes discussed above). These may be seen in action throughout chapter 6, in which the Chinese examples are written with SCs first: compare for instance the SC 'speech' radical, 讠 as it appears on the left side of a character, with the regular form 言; or the SC phonetic 义, standing for the old 義. In essence, these are the old cursive script-forms. What is new about them is their appearance as printed characters, though they are not yet completely universal and the regular forms are often found in their place, particularly when these stand alone without the addition of a second part. Among the radicals, three in

particular are variable, being found both in their traditional and simplified forms in communist texts: 发 *fā*: 'to start' (earlier 發, and still often met in that form); 门 *mén*: 'gate' (earlier 門); and 风 *fēng*: 'wind' (earlier 風).

Romanization

Western sinologists have a saying that when an appointment to a chair of Chinese is made, the new professor is expected to spend his first year inventing a new system of romanizing Chinese and the rest of his career battling for its adoption. The joke holds a certain grim relevance for the beginner. He must decide on one of the many rival systems as best suited to his needs. But, since he does not initially know what these needs are, nor what he will find easy or difficult in learning Chinese, his decision is a leap in the dark (he may of course be pushed, by group teacher or university department anxious for uniformity). By the time he can evaluate his choice, he may be thoroughly committed to it already, although an early change is often easy to make. Finally, aside from the absolute merits of different romanizations, there is the practical question of how much published material exists in each (see the following chapter).

Perhaps these very problems may encourage a correct spirit of robustness in the student. No romanization can teach flawless pronunciation. Very few Westerners ever acquire this, and the few who do so will spend many years in the Chinese world, possibly never studying by romanization at all. Even students less fortunately placed find romanization a tool to be discarded as soon as possible, or kept only for reference work; while specialist students will anyway need to be familiar with several systems, since they will meet books which use all of these.

Three questions should be asked (they seldom are) of a romanization:

(a) Does it take long to learn? Is the time required compatible with one's aim in studying Chinese?

(b) Does it read and write easily, or are marks, accents and superscript figures used continually?

(c) Does it lean towards 'eye-sound' spellings, or toward formalized, semi-symbolic uses of the roman letters? Which better suits one's own memorizing aptitude?

Answers given by the various systems must be highly subjective, but some facts and pointers may help.

Gwoyeu Romatzyh (GR) was designed (in 1926) by Chinese scholars, and promulgated (in 1928) by the Ministry of Education somewhat as a second runner to the *zhùyīn* phonetic alphabet. It scores on the questions as follows:

(a) Considerable time is needed to acquire thorough mastery of GR. Chao Yuen Ren, its chief architect, recommends in his *Mandarin Primer* that an initial hundred hours' practice be spent before meaning and syntax are even touched upon. By giving a different internal spelling to all vowels in all four tones, or where this is impossible then to initial or final consonants, GR forms a different visual image for each tonal sound in Mandarin. These may be found to impress themselves vividly on the memory, almost as do different words. If one's aim is to learn to speak Chinese, the value of this is clearly great, and the time given to basic phonetics needed to master GR will probably not prove wasted.

(b) It writes easily, and has no marks or accents. The system may be typed on a normal keyboard, and ordered alphabetically in lists or glossaries without too many of the same initial letters recurring. However, the visual impression of GR is ugly, that of a computer language with no spoken reality. Aversion to this could become an obstacle to progress.

(c) With certain syllables, GR's spellings are formalized away from the sound-value of the letters (e.g. with sounds in the second and fourth tones, which alter consonants). But since the system was designed expressly to make distinctions between tones, it is illogical to complain of the vividness of these, or that *jarng* (GR) is *less* easily perceived than is *jáng* (the *pīnyīn* spelling). The point under (b) will doubtless be clinching here. Students of written Chinese alone will probably not need GR's precision with tones, since the ideographs make a firm enough link with meanings in English.

[171]

Wade-Giles is the oldest and most widely used of all current romanizations, and its chief merit lies in this wide use. Students reading in history, geography and related subjects will find WG essential. They will meet its transcriptions in English publications, and will be expected to use it themselves when transliterating Chinese names.

(a) Learning-time, anyway quite long, will be increased by the many marks, accents and complex combinations of WG. For example, *sĭ* is written *ssŭ* in the complete transcription (often modified in use). WG is not worth learning as a 'first' system, since it is a cumbersome tool not generally followed in recently published text-books.

(b) Those whose Chinese is already advanced may find WG hard to read, since it distinguishes the aspirated and non-aspirated consonants by marks alone, hardly strong enough to spotlight meaningful differences. Beginners, going more slowly, may not find this a handicap. No one could claim that the system is easy to write.

(c) WG is highly formalized, e.g. it writes the 'French' *j*-sound for what is a retroflex *r*. This last may help with *jen*[2] (*rén*), but not e.g. with *jung*[2]-*i*[4]: 'easy', in which the sound is closer to *y*—. More helpful are the apostrophes for marks of aspiration. These emphasize the point that the consonant is the same whether aspirated or not, also that the change is not between voiced and unvoiced (as might be thought from a '*b/p*' romanization such as *pīnyīn*). Some students feel that the less the spelling is like 'English' the greater will be the attention focused on the Chinese sound; for such, WG is the answer. But in general it is not of real use until one is advanced enough with the language to read and transliterate on specialist subjects. As a starting-point for spoken Chinese it is unhelpful in that its hyphenation tends to stress the monosyllabic nature of script, and not the varying closeness of juncture in speech.

Yale arrived at their system soon after America's entry into World War II, which stimulated the study of oriental languages in the United States. It was designed to get quick results with home-based students learning spoken Chinese for service in the Far East.

(a) Yale can be learnt in a few hours, and so is valuable as a first romanization whatever the aim of study.

(b) The system reads easily, being phonetic overall rather than analytic of syllables in isolation. Its only marks are for the four tones. Compounds are written together, as words in connected speech, rather than linked as with WG's hyphens; compare Yale's *rúngyi*: 'easy' with Wade's *jung²-i⁴*. It has a preference for *w* and *y* (against *u/yu* and *i*) when these are in conjunction with other vowels. This is good in enabling compounds which 'join' at otherwise open vowels to be read correctly (as in *wūyā*: 'crow' for e.g. GR's *uia*); but it may also give too much weight to a semi-vowel, e.g. in *lwun* for *pīnyīn*'s *lün*, or *ywànyi* for *yùanyi*, which are not articulated in the same way as e.g. *wán*.

(c) All Yale's spellings are eye-sounds.

Pīnyīn has had a long evolution. Its origins are in Latinxua, a system devised and promulgated in the Soviet Far East in 1931, which was taken up in China (as Sin Wenz, or 'New Writing') some four years later. Ignored by the Kuomintang, it flourished in the communist-held north-west. In 1952 a research committee was formed to consider all aspects of the written language; after some experiments, the committee decided on *pīnyīn* (which differs from Latinxua mainly in spellings for certain guttural and palatal consonants, the final vowels being identical). Since 1958, *pīnyīn* has been the official system of the People's Republic.

(a) Arguably the quickest of all romanizations to learn, *pīnyīn* is particularly worth while in view of Peking's eventual plans for it.

(b) The system reads and writes easily, using fewer letters per sound than any other system. As used inside China, the tone-marks are not shown. This may prove a mistake when its use for Chinese native purposes is more widespread; foreign students should always write in the tone-marks. *Pīnyīn*'s only other mark is ·· over *u*, in the rounded *i* sound, often likewise not shown.

(c) *Pīnyīn* was of course designed for native users, but many foreigners feel that its balance between eye-sounds and symbolic spellings makes it ideal for Westerners. Two consonants are spelt with no regard for Western alphabet-values (*q* for the palatal *ch*, *x* for the palatal *sh*), and perhaps two more are only partly eye-sounds: *zh* for the retroflex *j*, *c* for the fricative *ts*. These are just the sounds which need special attention, so the use of symbols or part-symbols for them is appropriate. Elsewhere all are eye-sounds.

Booklist

For those wanting more on the background to reform, John DeFrancis's *Nationalism and Language Reform in China* (Princeton, 1950) goes into wider questions of politics, education and tradition; forceful views, clearly and often wittily expressed.

At the opposite extreme both in time and in linguistic theory is Bernhard Karlgren in his two short popularizing accounts of the earliest forms of script and their place in phonetics: *Sound and Symbol in Chinese* (Hong Kong and Oxford, rev. edn. 1962) and *The Chinese Language* (Ronald Press, 1949). The first of these much criticized for what it says of the modern language, but both should be read for their history.

Two more recent books offer the analysis of modern spoken Chinese into immediate constituents which this Pelican book has not attempted. Yuen Ren Chao's *A Grammar of Spoken Chinese* (U. of California, 1968) is the nearest approximation to a Chinese grammar of itself, in the sense of being entirely unexotic, but also takes its place as a classic in the modern linguistics of the West. Rigorous in method, but full of vitality and warmth. *The Chinese Language Today*, by Paul Kratochvil (Hutchinson, 1968), gives a framework in which the language may be discussed rather than actual pieces of Chinese to put into the frame. Complex terms from descriptive linguistics are used helpfully.

Those wishing to study modern Chinese for practical purposes, at whatever point on the scale between popular speech and semi-literary but still modern writing, will find the grid overleaf helpful. Numbers refer to books in the list that follows. The grid allows an immediate first sorting to be made by purpose of study and preference of romanization, and this should save time in which to look at other factors in choosing a book.

Recent years have brought much more of this type of publishing, and Yale's lead with their 'Mirror' series in the late 1950s is being challenged. But many books are now dated in idiom and subject-matter, and there is a need for more supplementary texts at second level. Also wanted is a Western-produced grammar of communist usage, and even more urgently a first-hand dictionary on comprehensive lines from simplified characters to English. There is almost nothing suitable to teach the language to secondary schools.

Comments on each book listed usually consider four factors: 1, the level of the text; 2, the number of characters involved (this tells one less than would the number of compounds a book teaches, but students always wish to know the former score); 3, the flavour of subject-matter in its excerpts or topic material; and 4, the way it presents grammar, if it does so at all.

With works giving speech and script-forms in one and the same book, chapter by chapter, no attempt is

	romanization only	characters only	speech with script	reference
GR	1* 11 12* 14 12+33	(1) (12) (14) (12)+33	30 31 32 33 1+(1)+31 12+(12) 14+(14)	37 44
Yale	2 6* 7* 8 9* 13 8+13+2/7	15* 16* 17* 20* 21* 25* 26 15+25 15, 16, 17, 25+26 (2) (6) (7) (13)	2+(2) 6+(6) 7+(7) 13+(13) 8+15, 16, 17	38 41 42 45 48
pīnyīn	3* 4* 5* 10*	22* 23* 24* 27 28 (3) (4) (5)	27 28 3+(3) 4+(4) } 22, 23, 24 5+(5)	40 46 47
Wade-Giles		18 19	29 34* 35	36 37 38 39 42 43

  * course with records or tapes
  + parallel courses
  ( ) character version of a romanized book

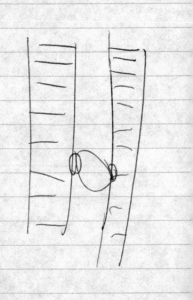

made here to say which is intended to come first for the student. Books in romanization only, however, whether or not they are followed by linked or parallel character-texts, must obviously give priority to speech. Except with reference books, dates are for the original edition.

Romanization only

1 *Mandarin Primer*. Yuen Ren Chao, Harvard U.P., 1948, viii + 336 pp; 1st level; character version exists; dialogues often very colloquial (some in dialect) which might dismay student seeking the norm; 27-page summary in Introduction is nucleus of author's classic 1968 *Grammar*; book expects much from user, who will also need a native teacher. See also **31**.

2 *A Sketch of Chinese Geography*. Charles C. J. Chu, Yale, Far Eastern Publications, 1954, xx + 218 pp; 2nd level; 20 lessons cover economics, population, mining, etc., with vocabulary of 1800 phrases assumed at start (drawn from **8** and **13**); notes and exercises; appendix of proper names has characters and a complete character version exists.

3 *Beginning Chinese*. John DeFrancis, Yale U.P., 1963, xxxi + 498 pp; 1st level, but this is the opening volume of eleven designed to provide the most comprehensive course available, over 2–3 years and up to 3rd level; chief features are extent and variety of drills, substitution tables, and games, also care-fully-tailored 'repeats' which ensure that a phrase or term is kept in use; story-line (American student in China) recurs in

4 *Intermediate Chinese* (1964, xii + 542 pp), as in

5 *Advanced Chinese* (1966, xvi + 574 pp), so that topics can range from situations in the family to sophisticated and quite technical lectures on e.g. Chinese literature, education, art, delivered at the student's Chinese university; overlaps and reviews remind of earlier volume material, and some sections can also be jumped (as for example from **3** to **5** via **22** and first chapters only of **23**). Use of English minimal, and decreases through series; separate character-texts exist, and see also the parallel 'Reader' volumes. Some later parts find it difficult to maintain zest and careful detail of earlier ones, but this is certainly the finest practical spoken course available.

6 *Talks on Chinese History*. John DeFrancis and Elizabeth Jen Young, Yale, Far Eastern Publications, 1952, xvi + 156 pp; 2nd level; three lectures, recorded as given to audience and then romanized, plus three dialogues (in 100 per cent colloquial style) on the material; this allows comparison of semi-literary with ordinary idiomatic usages; character version exists.

7 *A Sketch of Chinese History*. Henry C. Fenn, Yale, Far Eastern Publications, 1952, xx + 183 pp; designed (as **2**) to follow **8** and **13**; 28 lessons cover period from Shang to Manchu dynasty and the First Republic; maps and charts; complete vocabulary with characters at end; character version exists.

8 *Speak Mandarin*. Henry C. Fenn and M. Gardner Tewksbury, Yale U.P., 1967, xix + 238 pp; 1st level, keystone volume of Yale 'Mirror' series; re-working of Tewksbury's much-used *Speak Chinese* (Yale, 1948) but with more on phonology, larger total vocabulary despite fewer lessons, and livelier materials; grammar in notes; more compact, less drill-minded than **3**, but according to some users equally good. A *Student's Workbook* also exists (further drills and exercises).

9 *Spoken Chinese*. Charles F. Hockett and Chaoying Fang, Henry Holt, 1944, 2 vols in one: x + 231 and v + 232–617 pp; 1st level; near-Yale romanization; 30 units, each sixth one a review; topics cover everyday situations (e.g. telephoning), with many drills, some designed for group-work; grammar in notes;

practical course for services, with teacher assumed; rich in spoken examples, and a model in approach although somewhat dated in content.

10 *Introduction to Chinese* and *Speaking Chinese*. David Pollard, B.B.C. Publications, 1966 and 1967, 26 and 35 pp; 1st level; ten short lessons, in the simplest general conversational style, and a further fifteen in the second booklet, written to accompany two series of broadcasts intended to show the foreigner that speaking Chinese is possible for him; minimal grammar in notes; a recording of the sounds of Mandarin (not a transcript of the booklets) is also available; in the absence of material specially written for them, a most suitable introduction for secondary schools.

11 *Structure Drill in Chinese*. W. Simon and T. C. Chao, Lund Humphries, 1945, xi + 100 pp; 1st level; 50 sections, each of which has as its heading a common phrase (e.g. 'This — is not — but —') and 15 examples of it completed, so that by transposing material further instances can be made up; no grammar.

12 *Chinese Sentence Series*. W. Simon and C. H. Lu, Arthur Probsthain, 1942, vol. 1 (text) lxvi + 164 pp, vol. 2 (character version) 163 pp, vol. 3 (glossary) 49 pp; 1st level; may be used earlier than **33** (of which it is the parent work), as 'situations' begin with the very simplest; particularly good for verb-practice.

13 *Chinese Dialogues*. Fred Fang-yü Wang, Yale, Far Eastern Publications, 1953, vi + 385 pp; 1st level; designed to follow **8** (see also **2** and **7**); dialogues centre round a journey to Shanghai and are accompanied by notes on usage and structure, also drills and exercises; character version exists.

14 *Kuo-yü Lessons for Malayan Students*. T. M. Yang and R. Bruce, Government Publications, Kuala Lumpur, 1956, 227 pp; 1st level, perfectly acceptable for non-Malayan students; 30

lessons and 12 dialogues, the Malayan background and vocabulary-choice adding Far East flavour; grammar by examples, with a few good notes; character version exists.

Characters only (romanization in notes)

15 *Read Chinese* 1. Fang-yü Wang, Yale, Far Eastern Publications, 1953, xxiii + 236 pp; 1st level; 0–300 characters; short narratives and general topics; Introduction summarizes grammar; both this and **16** use 'rebus' method (romanization where a needed character is not yet known to student).

16 *Read Chinese* 2. Richard Chang, Yale, Far Eastern Publications, 1958, vii + 223 pp; 1st level; 300–600 characters; made-up narratives, connected; as with previous volume, excellent calligraphy.

17 *Read Chinese* 3. Richard Chang and Fang-yü Wang, Yale, Far Eastern Publications, 1961, xiv + 242 pp; 2nd level; 600–1000 characters: excerpts from communist and overseas press, and from pre-1949 books.

18 *Readings in Chinese Communist Documents.* Wen-shun Chi, U. of California Press, 1963, xvi + 478 pp; 3rd level; 15 major policy or 'for the record' statements 1949–54, photoprinted from the originals, with background and vocabulary for each; two glossaries (alphabetical and radical).

19 *Readings in Chinese Communist Ideology.* Wen-shun Chi, U. of California Press, 1968, x + 440 pp; 3rd level; 10 sections by topic, the first (100 pp) on Mao's Thought, others on e.g. law, the constitution, historiography, revisionism; Appendix converts simplified to regular characters, and *v.v.*

20 *A Primer of Newspaper Chinese.* Yu-ju Chih, Yale, Far Eastern Publications, 1956, ix + 245 pp; probably 3rd level;

800 characters assumed; 22 excerpts from overseas and communist press, dated but interesting in style, with supporting material on e.g. government structure, transliteration method used by newspapers; grammar in notes.

21 *Advanced Chinese Newspaper Readings*. Yu-ju Chih, Yale, Far Eastern Publications, 1960, ii + 163 pp; 3rd level; about 1500 characters assumed; 12 editorial-type articles mainly from communist press, notes on background, vocabulary and usage; some articles have simplified characters, but index is by regular stroke-count only.

22 *Beginning Chinese Reader*. John DeFrancis, Yale U.P., 1966, xxxii + 1004 pp (2 vols); for plan of series see under **3–5**; also gives simplified characters in supplementary lessons; rounds out and extends practice in the usages taught by the *Beginning Chinese* volume, as for their respective volumes do

23 *Intermediate Chinese Reader* (1967, xvi + 1427 pp, 2 vols) and

24 *Advanced Chinese Reader* (1968, xvi + 713 pp). The distribution of characters through the entire DeFrancis course (eight volumes in characters) may be set out thus: 494 in (**3**), plus 33 beyond this in **22**; 696 new characters in (**4**); 904 new characters in (**5**), beyond those in **22** and the first six lessons of **23**; and 400 new characters in **24**.

25 *Read About China*. Pao-ch'en Lee, Yale, Far Eastern Publications, 1958, x + 127 pp; assumes the characters of **15**, gives 300 beyond; 20 short texts on e.g. geography, history, Chinese inventions and customs, plus vocabulary and notes.

26 *Intermediate Reader in Modern Chinese*. Harriet C. Mills with P. S. Ni, Cornell U.P., 1967, vol. 1 (texts) xx + 270 pp, vols 2 and 3 xx + 366 and xi + 367–741 pp; 2nd and 3rd level; 1000–2000 characters; wide variety of texts, pre- and post-1949, the majority by communist writers; the two volumes of notes give very full details of vocabulary, use of characters and compounds in and out of context, grammar, and exercises on structures and translation.

27 *Modern Chinese Reader* (to be renamed 'Course'). No author given; compiled at the Chinese Language special course for foreign students, Peking University, 'Epoch' Publishing House, Peking, 1962, 2 vols, 786 pp; 1st level; 0–758 characters (simplified); texts have communist educational flavour, cover situations and usage likely to be met in mainland China; 72 lessons, each sixth one a review; grammar very detailed but cumbersome, given throughout in bilingual notes with full summary and probably meant as much for native Chinese instructor as for foreign pupil; good stroke-formation charts.

28 *Modern Chinese Readers* (note title). Authorship as above; The Commercial Press, Peking, 1964– , vol. 1 x + 149 pp, at 1st level. Both this volume and a published second (not seen) are intended to form part of a 4-year package: the two volumes of '*Modern Chinese Course*' (i.e. **27**) plus six 'Readers', giving a total of 3000 characters. In this first Reader are 18 lessons with texts consisting mainly of abridgements of longer works; grammar notes and exercises tie in with the Course itself.

Characters alongside romanization

29 *Elementary Chinese*. Shau Wing Chan, Stanford U.P., 1951, xxxi + 468 pp; 1st level; 0–845 characters, with some discussion of simplified characters in later edition; reading material in characters and romanization, oral and written exercises; grammar in notes.

30 *Chinese Conversation in the National Language*. T. C. Chao, Lund Humphries, 1947, vii + 120 pp; 1st level; 0–1034 characters, facing romanization and translation; 60 short dialogues, with a bias to sport but some on e.g. government, economics; useful as giving compact subject-vocabularies.

31 *A Syllabus for Mandarin Primer*. Rulan Chao Pian, Harvard U.P., 1960, ii + 116 pp; 1st level; about 1500 characters; by Y. R. Chao's daughter, this fills out his *Primer* (see **1**) with more instances, lesson by lesson, of structure and usage given without notes or further comment, and thus forms a kind of wordless grammar in itself.

32 1200 *Chinese Basic Characters*. Walter Simon, Lund Humphries, 1944, xvi + 334 pp; 1st level; 0–1269 characters; adaptation of 96 short 'situations' (e.g. writing a letter) issued in China as part of a mass education movement in the 1920s.

33 *Chinese Reader and Guide to Conversation*. W. Simon and C. H. Lu, Lund Humphries, 1943, viii + 196 pp; 1st level; 0–approx. 1200 characters; narrative of voyage to China, with short situations cumulatively building up vocabulary load ('Gouin' method); see also **12**.

34 *Conversational Chinese*. Têng Ssŭ-yü, Chicago U.P., 1947, xi + 441 pp; 1st level; 0–933 characters: conversations between several speakers, grouped by topic; grammar in notes, with some résumé chapters on e.g. the verb; inadequate treatment of script; romanizes with tone-marks, not figures.

35 *Advanced Conversational Chinese*. Têng Ssŭ-yü, Chicago U.P., 1965, xiv + 293 pp; 2nd level; about 1500 characters, mostly beyond those in **34**; conversations on e.g. politics, history, religion, also two excerpts from 20th-century plays.

Reference

36 *A Concise English-Chinese Dictionary*. Shau Wing Chan, Stanford U.P., 2nd edn. 1955, xvii + 416 pp; approx. 7000 headwords, few sub-entries and beginners would want more precision in them; mainly general vocabulary and conversational usage.

37 *Concise Dictionary of Spoken Chinese*. Yuen Ren Chao and Lien Sheng Yang, Harvard U.P., 1947, xxxix + 292 pp; approx. 5000 head entries, by character ordered under radical, many explanatory examples, with literary forms differentiated; attention to botany but little other science, bias being to general conversational usage; some pioneer morphological apparatus; more a check-list than a dictionary.

38 *Chinese Characters Easily Confused*. Henry C. Fenn, Yale, Far Eastern Publications, 1953, ii + 84 pp; approx. 800 characters, grouped by 276 similar shapes; a stroke-count index directs user to the appropriate group for the character needing to be distinguished.

39 *'Five Thousand' Dictionary* [Chinese-English]. C. H. Fenn, Harvard U.P. rev. edn. 1948, xxxviii + 696 pp (original edn. 1926); 5000 head characters, chosen by frequency-count, and entries which distinguish literary usage (but in this respect, as also that of frequency, doubtless dated); bias to biological sciences.

40 *A Modern Chinese–English Dictionary for Students*. C. C. Huang, Center for East Asian Studies, U. of Kansas, 1968, xix + 648 pp; 4500 head characters, alphabetically, with simplified after regular (but not in sub-entries); not enough given on the communist compounds which dictionary's basis assumes are being read; good index by total stroke-count of both simplified and regular character, cross-referred to entry by key-number; a useful interim simplified-character dictionary.

41 *Vocabulary of Spoken Chinese*. Po-fei Huang, Yale, Far Eastern Publications, 1954, xvi + 347 pp; approx. 9000 entries (headwords plus compounds) in the two sections, Chinese-English/English-Chinese; collates material from other Yale books (principally **8**, **13** and **25**); bias to services' vocabulary.

42 *Chinese Newspaper Manual.* Tien-yi Li, Yale, Far Eastern Publications, 1953, xxiv + 262 pp; information will be of most use to readers of overseas Chinese press: abbreviation forms, names of personalities, government departments (inc. comparative table, internationally), geographical terms; inevitably dated.

43 *Chinese–English Dictionary.* R. H. Mathews, Shanghai, 1931, rev. U.S. edn. Harvard U.P., 1943, xxiv + 1226 pp; 7785 head characters, with above 100,000 compounds or subentry phrases; indexed by radical and stroke-count; now very dated, and probably never adequate on the spoken idiom, it remains the one large dictionary that gives literary and historical forms at student level.

44 *A Beginners' Chinese–English Dictionary.* Walter Simon, Lund Humphries, 3rd rev. edn. 1964, cxl + 1074 pp; approx. 6000 head characters, alphabetically, and 15,000 compounds (in romanization only); entries reflect 'national language' style of 1930s and 40s; useful appendixed information of a literary kind.

45 *Introduction to Chinese Cursive Script.* Fang-yü Wang, Yale, Far Eastern Publications, 1958, xxx + 240 pp; 300 characters (those of **15**) exemplified in various cursive hands; good historical Introduction, 2-colour printing.

46 *A Concise English-Chinese Dictionary.* Zhang Qi-qun, Commercial Press, Peking, 1963, 22 + 1252 pp; 26,000 headwords; simplified characters; definitions as paraphrases rather than literal equivalents; science and technology account for about one-fifth of total entries; appendixes very full, including some which identify via pictures; dictionary is most useful as backwards check when translating a communist-read term into English.

47 *Chinese-English Dictionary of Modern Communist Chinese Usage*. No author given; published (1963) by the U.S. Department of Commerce *et al.* as an adaptation of the 1959 Peking-issued Chinese-German Dictionary, the characters reproduced photographically and their explanations translated and edited into English, viii + 845 pp; approx. 5000 head characters, alphabetically, 35,000 sub-entries; much traditional material as well as modernisms; good appendixes; confusing index (by 'modified radicals', 186 in all) must cut down time the dictionary saves as the only one to use simplified characters Chinese-English throughout.

48 *Dictionary of Spoken Chinese*. Staff of the Institute of Far Eastern Languages, Yale U.P., 1966, xxxix + 1071 pp; Chinese-English section (two-fifths of whole) lists above 2750 head characters alphabetically, with romanization, grammatical category, meaning, and examples; English-Chinese has head-words and sub-entries in romanization only; character-index; basis of compilation makes this usable for forms encountered in reading also, but principally a very sound tool for beginners in spoken Chinese.

Penguinews and *Penguins in Print*

Every month we issue an illustrated magazine, *Penguinews*. It's a lively guide to all the latest Penguins, Pelicans and Puffins, and always contains an article on a major Penguin author, plus other features of contemporary interest.

Penguinews is supplemented by *Penguins in Print*, a complete list of all the available Penguin titles – there are now over four thousand!

The cost is no more than the postage; so why not write for a free copy of this month's *Penguinews*? And if you'd like both publications sent for a year, just send us a cheque or a postal order for 30p (if you live in the United Kingdom) or 60p (if you live elsewhere), and we'll put you on our mailing list.

Dept EP, Penguin Books Ltd,
Harmondsworth, Middlesex

Note: *Penguinews* and *Penguins in Print* are not available in the U.S.A. or Canada.

Some Pelicans about China:

Red Star Over China

Edgar Snow

The first full account to reach the West of Mao Tse-tung and the Red armies – a classic now revised and enlarged to keep it completely up to date.

Red China Today

Edgar Snow

A detailed and absorbing study which shows China developing under Communist rule through 'enormous difficulties' towards nuclear power.

China Comes of Age

Jean-Pierre Brulé

Today more than one human being in four is Chinese. Jean-Pierre Brulé examines the Chinese challenge on five fronts: demographic, economic, commercial, military and nuclear.

Also available:

China Readings

Edited by Franz Schurmann and Orville Schell
Volume 1 – Imperial China
Volume 2 – Republican China
Volume 3 – Communist China

China in the year 2001

Han Suyin

Not for sale in the U.S.A. or Canada